Cram101 Textbook Outlines to accompany:

An Introduction To Theories Of Personality

Hergenhahn, Olson, 6th Edition

An Academic Internet Publishers (AIPI) publication (c) 2007.

Cram101 and Cram101.com are AIPI publications and services. All notes, highlights, reviews, and practice tests are prepared by AIPI for use in AIPI publications, all rights reserved.

You have a discounted membership at www.Cram101.com with this book.

Get all of the practice tests for the chapters of this textbook, and access in-depth reference material for writing essays and papers. Here is an example from a Cram101 Biology text:

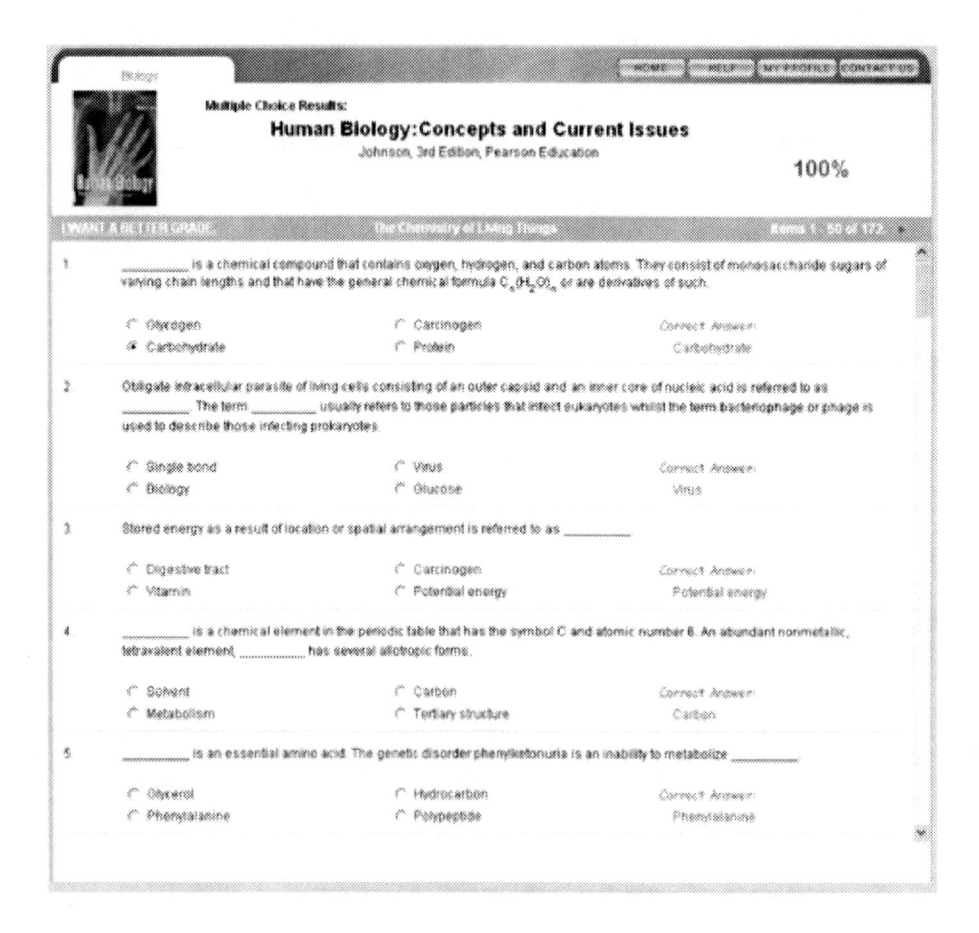

When you need problem solving help with math, stats, and other disciplines, www.Cram101.com will walk through the formulas and solutions step by step.

With Cram101.com online, you also have access to extensive reference material.

You will nail those essays and papers. Here is an example from a Cram101 Biology text:

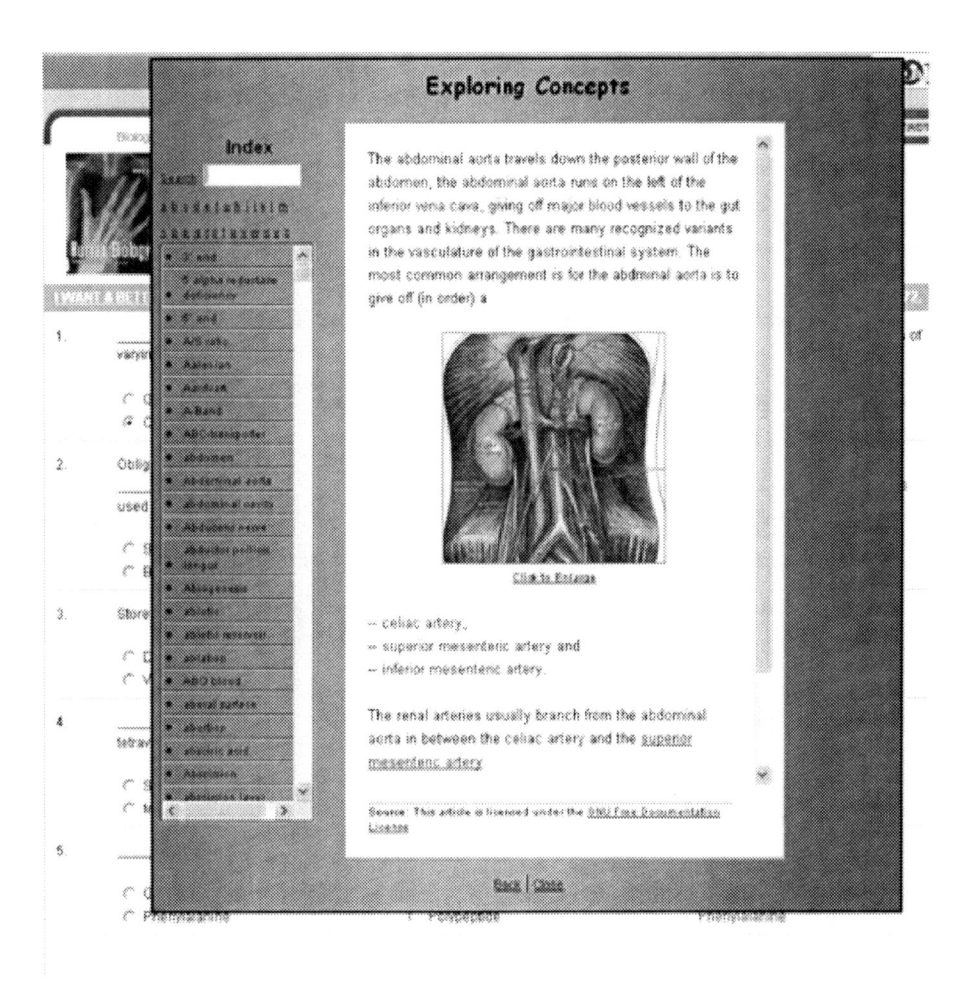

Visit **www.Cram101.com**, click Sign Up at the top of the screen, and enter DK73DW in the promo code box on the registration screen. Access to www.Cram101.com is normally $9.95, but because you have purchased this book, your access fee is only $4.95. Sign up and stop highlighting textbooks forever.

Learning System

Cram101 Textbook Outlines is a learning system. The notes in this book are the highlights of your textbook, you will never have to highlight a book again.

How to use this book. Take this book to class, it is your notebook for the lecture. The notes and highlights on the left hand side of the pages follow the outline and order of the textbook. All you have to do is follow along while your intructor presents the lecture. Circle the items emphasized in class and add other important information on the right side. With Cram101 Textbook Outlines you'll spend less time writing and more time listening. Learning becomes more efficient.

Cram101.com Online

Increase your studying efficiency by using Cram101.com's practice tests and online reference material. It is the perfect complement to Cram101 Textbook Outlines. Use self-teaching matching tests or simulate in-class testing with comprehensive multiple choice tests, or simply use Cram's true and false tests for quick review. Cram101.com even allows you to enter your in-class notes for an integrated studying format combining the textbook notes with your class notes.

Visit **www.Cram101.com**, click Sign Up at the top of the screen, and enter **DK73DW3460** in the promo code box on the registration screen. Access to www.Cram101.com is normally $9.95, but because you have purchased this book, your access fee is only $4.95. Sign up and stop highlighting textbooks forever.

Copyright © 2007 by Academic Internet Publishers, Inc. All rights reserved. "Cram101"® and "Never Highlight a Book Again!"® are registered trademarks of Academic Internet Publishers, Inc. The Cram101 Textbook Outline series is printed in the United States. ISBN: 1-4288-0301-7

An Introduction To Theories Of Personality
Hergenhahn, Olson, 6th

CONTENTS

1. What Is Personality? 2
2. Sigmund Freud 12
3. Carl Jung 32
4. Alfred Adler 44
5. Karen Horney 54
6. Erik H. Erikson 62
7. Gordon Allport 74
8. Raymond B. Cattell and Hans J. Eysenck 84
9. B. F. Skinner 102
10. John Dollard and Neal Miller 118
11. Albert Bandura and Walter Mischel 130
12. Edward O. Wilson 142
13. George Kelly 156
14. Carl Rogers 166
15. Abraham Maslow 176
16. Rollo Reese May 188
17. A Final Word 198

Chapter 1. What Is Personality?

Personality	Personality refers to the pattern of enduring characteristics that differentiates a person, the patterns of behaviors that make each individual unique.
Persona	In Jungian archetypal psychology, the Persona is the mask or appearance one presents to the world. It may appear in dreams under various guises.
Human nature	Human nature is the fundamental nature and substance of humans, as well as the range of human behavior that is believed to be invariant over long periods of time and across very different cultural contexts.
Gene	A gene is an ultramicroscopic area of the chromosome. It is the smallest physical unit of the DNA molecule that carries a piece of hereditary information.
Individual differences	Individual differences psychology studies the ways in which individual people differ in their behavior. This is distinguished from other aspects of psychology in that although psychology is ostensibly a study of individuals, modern psychologists invariably study groups.
Genetics	Genetics is the science of genes, heredity, and the variation of organisms.
Heredity	Heredity is the transfer of characteristics from parent to offspring through their genes.
Identical twins	Identical twins occur when a single egg is fertilized to form one zygote (monozygotic) but the zygote then divides into two separate embryos. The two embryos develop into foetuses sharing the same womb. Monozygotic twins are genetically identical unless there has been a mutation in development, and they are almost always the same gender.
Personality trait	According to the Diagnostic and Statistical Manual of the American Psychiatric Association, a personality trait is a "prominent aspect of personality that is exhibited in a wide range of important social and personal contexts. ...".
Questionnaire	A self-report method of data collection or clinical assessment method in which the individual being studied checks off items on a printed list, answers multiple-choice questions, or writes out answers to essay questions aimed at producing a selfdescription is called questionnaire.
Heritability	Heritability It is that proportion of the observed variation in a particular phenotype within a particular population, that can be attributed to the contribution of genotype. In other words: it measures the extent to which differences between individuals in a population are due their being different genetically.
Variable	A variable refers to a measurable factor, characteristic, or attribute of an individual or a system.
Nature-nurture	Nature-nurture is a shorthand expression for debates about the relative importance of an individual's "nature" versus personal experiences ("nurture") in determining or causing physical and behavioral traits.
Nativist	A nativist believes that certain skills or abilities are native or hard wired into the brain at birth.
Trait	An enduring personality characteristic that tends to lead to certain behaviors is called a trait. The term trait also means a genetically inherited feature of an organism.
Theories	Theories are logically self-consistent models or frameworks describing the behavior of a certain natural or social phenomenon. They are broad explanations and predictions concerning phenomena of interest.
Allport	Allport was a trait theorist. Those traits he believed to predominate a person's personality were called central traits. Traits such that one could be indentifed by the trait, were referred to as cardinal traits. Central traits and cardinal traits are influenced by environmental factors.
Society	The social sciences use the term society to mean a group of people that form a semi-closed (or semi-open) social system, in which most interactions are with other individuals belonging to the group.
Norms	In testing, standards of test performance that permit the comparison of one person's score on the test to the scores of others who have taken the same test are referred to as norms.

Chapter 1. What Is Personality?

Chapter 1. What Is Personality?

Adler	Adler argued that human personality could be explained teleologically, separate strands dominated by the guiding purpose of the individual's unconscious self ideal to convert feelings of inferiority to superiority (or rather completeness). The desires of the self ideal were countered by social and ethical demands.
Learning	Learning is a relatively permanent change in behavior that results from experience. Thus, to attribute a behavioral change to learning, the change must be relatively permanent and must result from experience.
Punishment	Punishment is the addtion of a stimulus that reduces the frequency of a response, or the removal of a stimulus that results in a reduction of the response.
Free association	In psychoanalysis, the uncensored uttering of all thoughts that come to mind is called free association.
Hypnosis	Hypnosis is a psychological state whose existence and effects are strongly debated. Some believe that it is a state under which the subject's mind becomes so suggestible that the hypnotist, the one who induces the state, can establish communication with the subconscious mind of the subject and command behavior that the subject would not choose to perform in a conscious state.
Unconscious mind	The unconscious mind refers to information processing and brain functioning of which a person is unaware. In Freudian theory, it is the repository of unacceptable thoughts and feelings.
Consciousness	The awareness of the sensations, thoughts, and feelings being experienced at a given moment is called consciousness.
Jung	Jung was in some aspects a response to Sigmund Freud's psychoanalysis. He proposed and developed the concepts of the extroverted and introverted personality, archetypes, and the collective unconscious. His work has been influential in psychiatry and in the study of religion, literature, and related fields.
Child development	Scientific study of the processes of change from conception through adolescence is called child development.
Motivation	In psychology, motivation is the driving force (desire) behind all actions of an organism.
Perception	Perception is the process of acquiring, interpreting, selecting, and organizing sensory information.
Pathology	Pathology is the study of the processes underlying disease and other forms of illness, harmful abnormality, or dysfunction.
Striving for superiority	According to Adler, the universal drive to adapt, improve oneself, and master life's challenges is referred to as striving for superiority.
Postulates	Postulates are general statements about behavior that cannot be directly verified. They are used to generate theorems which can be tested.
Ego	In Freud's view the Ego serves to balance our primitive needs and our moral beliefs and taboos. Relying on experience, a healthy Ego provides the ability to adapt to reality and interact with the outside world.
Skinner	Skinner conducted research on shaping behavior through positive and negative reinforcement, and demonstrated operant conditioning, a technique which he developed in contrast with classical conditioning.
Bandura	Bandura is best known for his work on social learning theory or Social Cognitivism. His famous Bobo doll experiment illustrated that people learn from observing others.
Mischel	Mischel is known for his cognitive social learning model of personality that focuses on the specific cognitive variables that mediate the manner in which new experiences affect the individual.
Maslow	Maslow is mostly noted today for his proposal of a hierarchy of human needs which he often presented as

Chapter 1. What Is Personality?

Chapter 1. What Is Personality?

a pyramid. Maslow was an instrumental player in the formation of the humanistic movement, also known as the third force in psychology.

Free will	The idea that human beings are capable of freely making choices or decisions is free will.
Determinism	Determinism is the philosophical proposition that every event, including human cognition and action, is causally determined by an unbroken chain of prior occurrences.
Introspection	Introspection is the self report or consideration of one's own thoughts, perceptions and mental processes. Classic introspection was done through trained observers.
Brain	The brain controls and coordinates most movement, behavior and homeostatic body functions such as heartbeat, blood pressure, fluid balance and body temperature. Functions of the brain are responsible for cognition, emotion, memory, motor learning and other sorts of learning. The brain is primarily made up of two types of cells: glia and neurons.
Idiographic	An idiographic investigation studies the characteristics of an individual in depth.
Nomothetic	Nomothetic measures are contrasted to ipsative or idiothetic measures, where nomothetic measures are measures that can be taken directly by an outside observer, such as weight or how many times a particular behavior occurs, and ipsative measures are self-reports such as a rank-ordered list of preferences.
Instinct	Instinct is the word used to describe inherent dispositions towards particular actions. They are generally an inherited pattern of responses or reactions to certain kinds of situations.
Humanistic	Humanistic refers to any system of thought focused on subjective experience and human problems and potentials.
Stimulus	A change in an environmental condition that elicits a response is a stimulus.
Habit	A habit is a response that has become completely separated from its eliciting stimulus. Early learning theorists used the term to describe S-R associations, however not all S-R associations become a habit, rather many are extinguished after reinforcement is withdrawn.
Rationalism	Rationalism is a philosophical doctrine that asserts that the truth should be determined by reason and factual analysis, rather than faith, dogma or religious teaching. Rationalism has some similarities in ideology and intent to humanism and atheism, in that it aims to provide a framework for social and philosophical discourse outside of religious or supernatural beliefs.
Reasoning	Reasoning is the act of using reason to derive a conclusion from certain premises. There are two main methods to reach a conclusion, deductive reasoning and inductive reasoning.
Rationalist	The rationalist movement is a philosophical doctrine that asserts that the truth can best be discovered by reason and factual analysis, rather than faith, dogma or religious teaching.
Empiricism	Empiricism is generally regarded as being at the heart of the modern scientific method, that our theories should be based on our observations of the world rather than on intuition, or deductive logic.
Empirical	Empirical means the use of working hypotheses which are capable of being disproved using observation or experiment.
Hypothesis	A specific statement about behavior or mental processes that is testable through research is a hypothesis.
Heuristic	A heuristic is a simple, efficient rule of thumb proposed to explain how people make decisions, come to judgments and solve problems, typically when facing complex problems or incomplete information. These rules work well under most circumstances, but in certain cases lead to systematic cognitive biases.
Repression	A defense mechanism, repression involves moving thoughts unacceptable to the ego into the unconscious, where they cannot be easily accessed.

Chapter 1. What Is Personality?

Chapter 1. What Is Personality?

Stages	Stages represent relatively discrete periods of time in which functioning is qualitatively different from functioning at other periods.
Psychophysics	Psychophysics refers to the study of the mathematical relationship between the physical aspects of stimuli and our psychological experience of them.
Cognition	The intellectual processes through which information is obtained, transformed, stored, retrieved, and otherwise used is cognition.
Testimonial	A testimonial or endorsement is a written or spoken statement, sometimes from a public figure, sometimes from a private citizen, extolling the virtue of some product, which is used in the promotion and advertising of that product.
Case study	A carefully drawn biography that may be obtained through interviews, questionnaires, and psychological tests is called a case study.
The Structure of Scientific Revolutions	The Structure of Scientific Revolutions is an analysis of the history of science. Its publication was a landmark event in the sociology of knowledge, and popularized the terms paradigm and paradigm shift.
Kuhn	Kuhn is most famous for his book The Structure of Scientific Revolutions in which he presented the idea that science does not evolve gradually toward truth, but instead undergoes periodic revolutions which he calls "paradigm shifts."
Paradigm	Paradigm refers to the set of practices that defines a scientific discipline during a particular period of time. It provides a framework from which to conduct research, it ensures that a certain range of phenomena, those on which the paradigm focuses, are explored thoroughly. It may also blind scientists to other, perhaps more fruitful, ways of dealing with their subject matter.
Psychoanalytic	Freud's theory that unconscious forces act as determinants of personality is called psychoanalytic theory. The theory is a developmental theory characterized by critical stages of development.
Psyche	Psyche is the soul, spirit, or mind as distinguished from the body. In psychoanalytic theory, it is the totality of the id, ego, and superego, including both conscious and unconscious components.
Learning paradigm	In abnormal psychology, the set of assumptions that abnormal behavior is learned in the same way as other human behavior is a learning paradigm.
Free choice	Free choice refers to the ability to freely make choices that are not controlled by genetics, learning, or unconscious forces.
Popper	Popper proposed a set of methodological rules called Falsificationism. Falsificationism is the idea that science advances by unjustified, exaggerated guesses followed by unstinting criticism. Only hypotheses capable of clashing with observation reports are allowed to count as scientific. Falsifiable theories enhance our control over error while expanding the richness of what we can say about the world.
Falsifiability	According to Popper the extent to which a scientific assertion is amenable to systematic probes, any one of which could negate the scientist's expectations is referred to as falsifiability.
Astrology	Astrology is any of several traditions or systems in which knowledge of the apparent positions of celestial bodies is held to be useful in understanding, interpreting, and organizing knowledge about human existence.
Reaction formation	In Freud's psychoanalytic theory, reaction formation is a defense mechanism in which anxiety-producing or unacceptable emotions are replaced by their direct opposites.
Scientific method	Psychologists gather data in order to describe, understand, predict, and control behavior. Scientific method refers to an approach that can be used to discover accurate information. It includes these steps: understand the problem, collect data, draw conclusions, and revise research conclusions.

Chapter 1. What Is Personality?

Chapter 1. What Is Personality?

Gender difference	A gender difference is a disparity between genders involving quality or quantity. Though some gender differences are controversial, they are not to be confused with sexist stereotypes.
Overt behavior	An action or response that is directly observable and measurable is an overt behavior.
Emotion	An emotion is a mental states that arise spontaneously, rather than through conscious effort. They are often accompanied by physiological changes.
Lorenz	Lorenz demonstrated how incubator-hatched geese would imprint on the first suitable moving stimulus they saw within what he called a "critical period" of about 36 hours shortly after hatching. Most famously, the goslings would imprint on Lorenz himself.
Plato	According to Plato, people must come equipped with most of their knowledge and need only hints and contemplation to complete it. Plato suggested that the brain is the mechanism of mental processes and that one gained knowledge by reflecting on the contents of one's mind.
Kant	Kant held that all known objects are phenomena of consciousness and not realities of the mind. But, the known object is not a mere bundle of sensations for it includes unsensational characteristics or manifestation of a priori principles. He insisted that the scientist and the philosopher approached nature with certain implicit principles, and Kant saw his task to be that of finding and making explicit these principles.
Epistemology	Epistemology is the branch of philosophy that deals with the nature, origin and scope of knowledge.
Mind-body problem	There are three basic views of the mind-body problem: mental and physical events are totally different, and cannot be reduced to each other (dualism); mental events are to be reduced to physical events (materialism); and physical events are to be reduced to mental events (phenomenalism).
Monism	Monism is the metaphysical view that there is only one principle, essence, substance or energy.

Chapter 1. What Is Personality?

Chapter 2. Sigmund Freud

Self-esteem	Self-esteem refers to a person's subjective appraisal of himself or herself as intrinsically positive or negative to some degree.
Darwin	Darwin achieved lasting fame as originator of the theory of evolution through natural selection. His book Expression of Emotions in Man and Animals is generally considered the first text on comparative psychology.
Evolution	Commonly used to refer to gradual change, evolution is the change in the frequency of alleles within a population from one generation to the next. This change may be caused by different mechanisms, including natural selection, genetic drift, or changes in population (gene flow).
Instinct	Instinct is the word used to describe inherent dispositions towards particular actions. They are generally an inherited pattern of responses or reactions to certain kinds of situations.
Human nature	Human nature is the fundamental nature and substance of humans, as well as the range of human behavior that is believed to be invariant over long periods of time and across very different cultural contexts.
Sigmund Freud	Sigmund Freud was the founder of the psychoanalytic school, based on his theory that unconscious motives control much behavior, that particular kinds of unconscious thoughts and memories are the source of neurosis, and that neurosis could be treated through bringing these unconscious thoughts and memories to consciousness in psychoanalytic treatment.
Authoritarian	The term authoritarian is used to describe a style that enforces strong and sometimes oppressive measures against those in its sphere of influence, generally without attempts at gaining their consent.
Ernest Jones	Ernest Jones was arguably the best-known follower of Freud. His writings on the subject of psychoanalysis prompted him to launch The International Journal of Psychoanalysis in 1920.
Psychoanalysis	Psychoanalysis refers to the school of psychology that emphasizes the importance of unconscious motives and conflicts as determinants of human behavior. It was Freud's method of exploring human personality.
Kanner	Kanner was known for his work related to autism. He was the first physician in the United States to be identified as a child psychiatrist and his first textbook, Child Psychiatry in 1935, was the first English language textbook to focus on the psychiatric problems of children.
Scientific research	Research that is objective, systematic, and testable is called scientific research.
Cocaine	Cocaine is a crystalline tropane alkaloid that is obtained from the leaves of the coca plant. It is a stimulant of the central nervous system and an appetite suppressant, creating what has been described as a euphoric sense of happiness and increased energy.
Depression	In everyday language depression refers to any downturn in mood, which may be relatively transitory and perhaps due to something trivial. This is differentiated from Clinical depression which is marked by symptoms that last two weeks or more and are so severe that they interfere with daily living.
Local anesthetic	Local anesthetic drugs act mainly by inhibiting sodium influx through sodium-specific ion channels in the neuronal cell membrane, in particular the so-called voltage-gated sodium channels. When the influx of sodium is interrupted, an action potential cannot arise and signal conduction is thus inhibited.
Stimulant	A stimulant is a drug which increases the activity of the sympathetic nervous system and produces a sense of euphoria or awakeness.
Morphine	Morphine, the principal active agent in opium, is a powerful opioid analgesic drug. According

Chapter 2. Sigmund Freud

Chapter 2. Sigmund Freud

	to recent research, it may also be produced naturally by the human brain. Morphine is usually highly addictive, and tolerance and physical and psychological dependence develop quickly.
Sensation	Sensation is the first stage in the chain of biochemical and neurologic events that begins with the impinging of a stimulus upon the receptor cells of a sensory organ, which then leads to perception, the mental state that is reflected in statements like "I see a uniformly blue wall."
Addiction	Addiction is an uncontrollable compulsion to repeat a behavior regardless of its consequences. Many drugs or behaviors can precipitate a pattern of conditions recognized as addiction, which include a craving for more of the drug or behavior, increased physiological tolerance to exposure, and withdrawal symptoms in the absence of the stimulus.
Nicotine	Nicotine is an organic compound, an alkaloid found naturally throughout the tobacco plant, with a high concentration in the leaves. It is a potent nerve poison and is included in many insecticides. In lower concentrations, the substance is a stimulant and is one of the main factors leading to the pleasure and habit-forming qualities of tobacco smoking.
Charcot	Charcot took an interest in the malady then called hysteria. It seemed to be a mental disorder with physical manifestations, of immediate interest to a neurologist. He believed that hysteria was the result of a weak neurological system which was hereditary.
Neurologist	A physician who studies the nervous system, especially its structure, functions, and abnormalities is referred to as neurologist.
Attitude	An enduring mental representation of a person, place, or thing that evokes an emotional response and related behavior is called attitude.
Mesmer	Mesmer discovered what he called animal magnetism and others often called mesmerism. The evolution of Mesmer's ideas and practices led James Braid to develop hypnosis in 1842.
Hysteria	Hysteria is a diagnostic label applied to a state of mind, one of unmanageable fear or emotional excesses. The fear is often centered on a body part, most often on an imagined problem with that body part.
Uterus	The uterus or womb is the major female reproductive organ. The main function of the uterus is to accept a fertilized ovum which becomes implanted into the endometrium, and derives nourishment from blood vessels which develop exclusively for this purpose.
Hypnosis	Hypnosis is a psychological state whose existence and effects are strongly debated. Some believe that it is a state under which the subject's mind becomes so suggestible that the hypnotist, the one who induces the state, can establish communication with the subconscious mind of the subject and command behavior that the subject would not choose to perform in a conscious state.
Amnesia	Amnesia is a condition in which memory is disturbed. The causes of amnesia are organic or functional. Organic causes include damage to the brain, through trauma or disease, or use of certain (generally sedative) drugs.
Breuer	Breuer is perhaps best known for his work with Anna O. – a woman suffering with symptoms of paralysis, anaesthesias, and disturbances of vision and speech. The discussions of Anna O. between Freud and Breuer were documented in their Studies in Hysteria and became a formative basis of Freudian theory and psychoanalytic practice.
Friendship	The essentials of friendship are reciprocity and commitment between individuals who see themselves more or less as equals. Interaction between friends rests on a more equal power base than the interaction between children and adults.
Hallucination	A hallucination is a sensory perception experienced in the absence of an external stimulus, as distinct from an illusion, which is a misperception of an external stimulus. They may

Go to **Cram101.com** for the Practice Tests for this Chapter.

Chapter 2. Sigmund Freud

	occur in any sensory modality - visual, auditory, olfactory, gustatory, tactile, or mixed.
Catharsis	Catharsis has been adopted by modern psychotherapy as the act of giving expression to deep emotions often associated with events in the individuals past which have never before been adequately expressed.
Aristotle	Aristotle can be credited with the development of the first theory of learning. He concluded that ideas were generated in consciousness based on four principlesof association: contiguity, similarity, contrast, and succession. In contrast to Plato, he believed that knowledge derived from sensory experience and was not inherited.
Transference	Transference is a phenomenon in psychology characterized by unconscious redirection of feelings from one person to another.
Free association	In psychoanalysis, the uncensored uttering of all thoughts that come to mind is called free association.
Psychoanalytic	Freud's theory that unconscious forces act as determinants of personality is called psychoanalytic theory. The theory is a developmental theory characterized by critical stages of development.
Mental disorder	Mental disorder refers to a disturbance in a person's emotions, drives, thought processes, or behavior that involves serious and relatively prolonged distress and/or impairment in ability to function, is not simply a normal response to some event or set of events in the person's environment.
The Interpretation of Dreams	The Interpretation of Dreams is a book by Sigmund Freud. The book introduces the Id, the Ego, and the Superego, and describes Freud's theory of the unconscious with respect to Dream interpretation. Widely considered to be his most important contribution to Psychology.
Stanley Hall	His laboratory at Johns Hopkins is considered to be the first American laboratory of psychology. In 1887 Stanley Hall founded the American Journal of Psychology. His interests centered around child development and evolutionary theory
Habit	A habit is a response that has become completely separated from its eliciting stimulus. Early learning theorists used the term to describe S-R associations, however not all S-R associations become a habit, rather many are extinguished after reinforcement is withdrawn.
Society	The social sciences use the term society to mean a group of people that form a semi-closed (or semi-open) social system, in which most interactions are with other individuals belonging to the group.
Biological needs	Beyond physiological needs for survival, the next level are motivations that have an obvious biological basis but are not required for the immediate survival of the organism. These biological needs include the powerful motivations for sex, parenting and aggression.
Libido	Sigmund Freud suggested that libido is the instinctual energy or force that can come into conflict with the conventions of civilized behavior. Jung, condidered the libido as the free creative, or psychic, energy an individual has to put toward personal development, or individuation.
Eros	In Freudian psychology, Eros is the life instinct innate in all humans. It is the desire to create life and favours productivity and construction. Eros battles against the destructive death instinct of Thanatos.
Death instinct	The death instinct was defined by Sigmund Freud, in Beyond the Pleasure Principle(1920). It speculated on the existence of a fundamental death wish or death instinct, referring to an individual's own need to die.
Thanatos	In psychoanalytical theory, Thanatos is the death instinct, which opposes Eros. The "death

Chapter 2. Sigmund Freud

Chapter 2. Sigmund Freud

	instinct" identified by Sigmund Freud, which signals a desire to give up the struggle of life and return to quiescence and the grave.
Schopenhauer	For Schopenhauer, human will had ontological primacy over the intellect; in other words, desire is understood to be prior to thought, and, in a parallel sense, will is said to be prior to being.
Superego	Frued's third psychic structure, which functions as a moral guardian and sets forth high standards for behavior is the superego.
Ego	In Freud's view the Ego serves to balance our primitive needs and our moral beliefs and taboos. Relying on experience, a healthy Ego provides the ability to adapt to reality and interact with the outside world.
Wish fulfillment	A primitive method used by the id to attempt to gratify basic instincts is referred to as wish fulfillment.
Reflex	A simple, involuntary response to a stimulus is referred to as reflex. Reflex actions originate at the spinal cord rather than the brain.
Lamarck	Lamarck proposed a theory of evolution based on the idea that individuals adapt during their own lifetimes and transmit traits they acquire to their offspring, the "inheritance of acquired traits." In spite of its being largely discredited, Darwin and others acknowledged him as an early proponent of ideas about evolution.
Personality	Personality refers to the pattern of enduring characteristics that differentiates a person, the patterns of behaviors that make each individual unique.
Primary process	The primary process in psychoanalytic theory, is one of the id's means of reducing tension by imagining what it desires.
Reality principle	The reality principle tells us to subordinate pleasure to what needs to be done. Subordinating the pleasure principle to the reality principle is done through a psychological process Freud calls sublimation, where you take desires that can't be fulfilled, or shouldn't be fulfilled, and turn their energy into something useful and productive.
Reality testing	Reality testing is the capacity to perceive one's environment and oneself according to accurate sensory impressions.
Punishment	Punishment is the addtion of a stimulus that reduces the frequency of a response, or the removal of a stimulus that results in a reduction of the response.
Anxiety	Anxiety is a complex combination of the feeling of fear, apprehension and worry often accompanied by physical sensations such as palpitations, chest pain and/or shortness of breath.
Guilt	Guilt describes many concepts related to a negative emotion or condition caused by actions which are believed to be, morally wrong. According to Freud, the avoidance of guilt is the basis for moral behavior.
Super-ego	The Super-ego stands in opposition to the desires of the Id. The Super-ego is based upon the internalization of the world view, norms and mores a child absorbs from parents and the surrounding environment at a young age. As the conscience, it includes our sense of right and wrong, maintaining taboos specific to a child's internalization of parental culture.
Anticathexis	In psychoanalysis, Anticathexis is the energy derived from the Superego to run the Ego, according to Freud. The function of the anticathexis is to restrict and block cathexis from the Id for overall benefit.
Physiology	The study of the functions and activities of living cells, tissues, and organs and of the physical and chemical phenomena involved is referred to as physiology.

Chapter 2. Sigmund Freud

Chapter 2. Sigmund Freud

Helmholtz	Helmholtz a pioneer of the new science of psychology, was a rigorous experimental physiologist and philospher. He gave us the distinction betwen sensation and peception and is well known for his theories of color perception and hearing.
Cathexis	Tolman's cathexis is the acquisition of a connection between a given goal object and the corresponding drive for it.
Positivism	Positivism is an approach to understanding the world based on science. It can be traced back to Auguste Comte in the 19th century. Positivists believe that there is little if any methodological difference between social sciences and natural sciences; societies, like nature, operate according to laws.
Principle of conservation	The knowledge that the quantity of a substance remains the same even though its shape or other aspects of its physical appearance might change is the principle of conservation.
Neurotic anxiety	Neurotic anxiety refers to, in psychoanalytic theory, a fear of the consequences of expressing previously punished and repressed id impulses; more generally, unrealistic fear.
Moral anxiety	In psychoanalytic theory, the ego's fear of punishment for failure to adhere to the superego's standards of proper conduct is referred to as moral anxiety.
Repression	A defense mechanism, repression involves moving thoughts unacceptable to the ego into the unconscious, where they cannot be easily accessed.
Physiological needs	The easiest kinds of motivation to analyse, at least superficially, are those based upon obvious physiological needs. These include hunger, thirst, and escape from pain.
Primary drive	A primary drive is a state of tension or arousal arising from a biological or innate need; it is one not based on learning. A primary drive activates behavior.
Incest	Incest refers to sexual relations between close relatives, most often between daughter and father or between brother and sister.
Consciousness	The awareness of the sensations, thoughts, and feelings being experienced at a given moment is called consciousness.
Dream analysis	Dream analysis is a part of psychoanalysis that intends to look beneath the manifest content of a dream, i.e., what we perceive in the dream, to the latent content of a dream, i.e., the meaning of the dream and the reason we dreamt it.
Unconscious mind	The unconscious mind refers to information processing and brain functioning of which a person is unaware. In Freudian theory, it is the repository of unacceptable thoughts and feelings.
Displacement	An unconscious defense mechanism in which the individual directs aggressive or sexual feelings away from the primary object to someone or something safe is referred to as displacement. Displacement in linguistics is simply the ability to talk about things not present.
Sublimation	Sublimation is a coping mechanism. It refers to rechanneling sexual or aggressive energy into pursuits that society considers acceptable or admirable.
Denial	Denial is a psychological defense mechanism in which a person faced with a fact that is uncomfortable or painful to accept rejects it instead, insisting that it is not true despite what may be overwhelming evidence.
Projection	Attributing one's own undesirable thoughts, impulses, traits, or behaviors to others is referred to as projection.
Reaction formation	In Freud's psychoanalytic theory, reaction formation is a defense mechanism in which anxiety-producing or unacceptable emotions are replaced by their direct opposites.
Rationalization	Rationalization is the process of constructing a logical justification for a decision that

Chapter 2. Sigmund Freud

Chapter 2. Sigmund Freud

	was originally arrived at through a different mental process. It is one of Freud's defense mechanisms.
Affect	A subjective feeling or emotional tone often accompanied by bodily expressions noticeable to others is called affect.
Emotion	An emotion is a mental states that arise spontaneously, rather than through conscious effort. They are often accompanied by physiological changes.
Psychosexual stages	In Freudian theory each child passes through five psychosexual stages. During each stage, the id focuses on a distinct erogenous zone on the body. Suffering from trauma during any of the first three stages may result in fixation in that stage. Freud related the resolutions of the stages with adult personalities and personality disorders.
Stages	Stages represent relatively discrete periods of time in which functioning is qualitatively different from functioning at other periods.
Erogenous zone	An erogenous zone is an area of the human body that has heightened sensitivity and stimulation normally results in sexual response.
Fixation	Fixation in abnormal psychology is the state where an individual becomes obsessed with an attachment to another human, animal or inanimate object. Fixation in vision refers to maintaining the gaze in a constant direction. .
Oral stage	The oral stage in psychology is the term used by Sigmund Freud to describe the development during the first eighteen months of life, in which an infant's pleasure centers are in the mouth. This is the first of Freud's psychosexual stages.
Anal stage	The anal stage in psychology is the term used by Sigmund Freud to describe the development during the second year of life, in which a child's pleasure and conflict centers are in the anal area.
Enuresis	Enuresis is involuntary urination while asleep. It is the normal state of affairs in infancy, but can be a source of embarrassment when it persists into school age or the teen years.
Parsimony	In science, parsimony is preference for the least complicated explanation for an observation. This is generally regarded as good when judging hypotheses. Occam's Razor also states the "principle of parsimony".
Phallic stage	The phallic stage is the 3rd of Freud's psychosexual stages, when awareness of and manipulation of the genitals is supposed to be a primary source of pleasure. In this stage the child deals with the Oedipus complex, if male, or the Electra Complex, if female.
Masturbation	Masturbation is the manual excitation of the sexual organs, most often to the point of orgasm. It can refer to excitation either by oneself or by another, but commonly refers to such activities performed alone.
Clitoris	Clitoris refers to an external female sex organ that is highly sensitive to sexual stimulation.
Penis	The penis is the external male copulatory organ and the external male organ of urination. In humans, the penis is homologous to the female clitoris, as it develops from the same embryonic structure. It is capable of erection for use in copulation.
Oedipus complex	The Oedipus complex is a concept developed by Sigmund Freud to explain the maturation of the infant boy through identification with the father and desire for the mother.
Castration anxiety	Castration anxiety is a fear posited by Sigmund Freud in his writings on the Oedipus complex at the genital stage of sexual development. It asserts that boys seeing a girl's genitalia will falsely assume that the girl must have had her penis removed, probably as punishment for some misbehavior, and will be anxious lest the same happen to him.

Chapter 2. Sigmund Freud

Chapter 2. Sigmund Freud

Castration	Castration is any action, surgical, chemical or otherwise, by which a biological male loses use of the testes. This causes sterilization, i.e. prevents him from reproducing; it also greatly reduces the production of certain hormones, such as testosterone.
Electra complex	A conflict of the phallic stage in which the girl longs for her father and resents her mother is called the Electra complex.
Bisexuality	Bisexuality is a sexual orientation characterized by aesthetic attraction, romantic love and sexual desire for both males and females.
Homosexuality	Homosexuality refers to a sexual orientation characterized by aesthetic attraction, romantic love, and sexual desire exclusively for members of the same sex or gender identity.
Homosexual	Homosexual refers to a sexual orientation characterized by aesthetic attraction, romantic love, and sexual desire exclusively for members of the same sex or gender identity.
Masculinity	Masculinity is a culturally determined value reflecting the set of characteristics of maleness.
Regression	Return to a form of behavior characteristic of an earlier stage of development is called regression.
Latency stage	Sigmund Freud suggested that the latency stage, age 6-10, this was a time of sexual latency, when the healthy child ceased all sexual interest and was vulnerable to trauma if he or she experienced sexuality.
Gender difference	A gender difference is a disparity between genders involving quality or quantity. Though some gender differences are controversial, they are not to be confused with sexist stereotypes.
Anatomy	Anatomy is the branch of biology that deals with the structure and organization of living things. It can be divided into animal anatomy (zootomy) and plant anatomy (phytonomy). Major branches of anatomy include comparative anatomy, histology, and human anatomy.
Heterosexuality	Sexual attraction and behavior directed to the opposite sex is heterosexuality.
Psychoanalyst	A psychoanalyst is a specially trained therapist who attempts to treat the individual by uncovering and revealing to the individual otherwise subconscious factors that are contributing to some undesirable behavior.
Karen Horney	Karen Horney, a neo-Freudian, deviated from orthodox Freudian analysis by emphasizing environmental and cultural, rather than biological, factors in neurosis.
Femininity	Femininity is the set of characteristics defined by a culture for idealized females.
Insight	Insight refers to a sudden awareness of the relationships among various elements that had previously appeared to be independent of one another.
Dream symbols	Images in dreams whose personal or emotional meanings differ from their literal meanings are called dream symbols.
Species	Species refers to a reproductively isolated breeding population.
Secondary elaboration	Making a dream more logical and complete while remembering it is a secondary elaboration.
Manifest content	In psychodynamic theory, the reported content of dreams is referred to as manifest content.
Latent content	In psychodynamic theory, the symbolized or underlying content of dreams is called latent content.
Freudian slip	The Freudian slip is named after Sigmund Freud, who described the phenomenon he called faulty action in his 1901 book The Psychopathology of Everyday Life. The Freudian slip is an error in human action, speech or memory that is believed to be caused by the unconscious mind.

Go to **Cram101.com** for the Practice Tests for this Chapter.

Chapter 2. Sigmund Freud

Chapter 2. Sigmund Freud

Motives	Needs or desires that energize and direct behavior toward a goal are motives.
Zimbardo	Zimbardo is best-known for his Stanford prison experiment. The experiment led to theories about the importance of the social situation in individual psychology that are still controversial today.
Symbolization	In Bandura's social cognitive theory, the ability to think about one's social behavior in terms of words and images is referred to as symbolization. Symbolization allows us to translate a transient experience into a guide for future action.
Wisdom	Wisdom is the ability to make correct judgments and decisions. It is an intangible quality gained through experience. Whether or not something is wise is determined in a pragmatic sense by its popularity, how long it has been around, and its ability to predict against future events.
Illusion	An illusion is a distortion of a sensory perception.
Seduction theory	Freud believed that all hyseria was traceable to sexual seduction and abuse. This theory, known as the seduction theory, he later modified and replaced with a psychoanalytic alternative, hysteria.
Loftus	Loftus works on human memory and how it can be changed by facts, ideas, suggestions and other forms of post-event information. One of her famous studies include the "car accident" study, which was an example of the misinformation effect.
Trauma	Trauma refers to a severe physical injury or wound to the body caused by an external force, or a psychological shock having a lasting effect on mental life.
American Psychological Association	The American Psychological Association is a professional organization representing psychology in the US. The mission statement is to "advance psychology as a science and profession and as a means of promoting health, education , and human welfare".
Sexual abuse	Sexual abuse is a term used to describe non- consentual sexual relations between two or more parties which are considered criminally and/or morally offensive.
False memory	A false memory is a memory of an event that did not happen or is a distortion of an event that did occur as determined by externally corroborated facts.
Syndrome	The term syndrome is the association of several clinically recognizable features, signs, symptoms, phenomena or characteristics which often occur together, so that the presence of one feature indicates the presence of the others.
Discrimination	In Learning theory, discrimination refers the ability to distinguish between a conditioned stimulus and other stimuli. It can be brought about by extensive training or differential reinforcement. In social terms, it is the denial of privileges to a person or a group on the basis of prejudice.
Prejudice	Prejudice in general, implies coming to a judgment on the subject before learning where the preponderance of the evidence actually lies, or formation of a judgement without direct experience.
Pathology	Pathology is the study of the processes underlying disease and other forms of illness, harmful abnormality, or dysfunction.
Statistics	Statistics is a type of data analysis which practice includes the planning, summarizing, and interpreting of observations of a system possibly followed by predicting or forecasting of future events based on a mathematical model of the system being observed.
Theories	Theories are logically self-consistent models or frameworks describing the behavior of a certain natural or social phenomenon. They are broad explanations and predictions concerning phenomena of interest.

Go to **Cram101.com** for the Practice Tests for this Chapter.

Chapter 2. Sigmund Freud

Chapter 2. Sigmund Freud

Empirical	Empirical means the use of working hypotheses which are capable of being disproved using observation or experiment.
Motivation	In psychology, motivation is the driving force (desire) behind all actions of an organism.
Psychopathology	Psychopathology refers to the field concerned with the nature and development of mental disorders.
Antecedents	In behavior modification, events that typically precede the target response are called antecedents.
Abnormal behavior	An action, thought, or feeling that is harmful to the person or to others is called abnormal behavior.
Ego ideal	The component of the superego that involves ideal standards approved by parents is called ego ideal. The ego ideal rewards the child by conveying a sense of pride and personal value when the child acts according to ideal standards.
Displaced aggression	Redirecting aggression to a target other than the actual source of one's frustration is a defense mechanism called displaced aggression.
Anna Freud	Anna Freud was a pioneer of child psychoanalysis. She popularized the notion that adolescence is a period that includes rapid mood fluctuation with enormous uncertainty about self.
Trait	An enduring personality characteristic that tends to lead to certain behaviors is called a trait. The term trait also means a genetically inherited feature of an organism.
Anal-expulsive	Anal-expulsive is characterized by being reckless, careless, defiant, disorganized.
Genital stage	The genital stage in psychology is the term used by Sigmund Freud to describe the final stage of human psychosexual development. It is characterized by the expression of libido through intercourse with an adult of the other gender.
Attention	Attention is the cognitive process of selectively concentrating on one thing while ignoring other things. Psychologists have labeled three types of attention: sustained attention, selective attention, and divided attention.
Parapraxes	Parapraxes or Freudian slip is an error in human action, speech or memory that is believed to be caused by the unconscious mind. The error often appears to the observer as being casual, bizarre or nonsensical.
Sympathetic	The sympathetic nervous system activates what is often termed the "fight or flight response". It is an automatic regulation system, that is, one that operates without the intervention of conscious thought.
Pupil	In the eye, the pupil is the opening in the middle of the iris. It appears black because most of the light entering it is absorbed by the tissues inside the eye. The size of the pupil is controlled by involuntary contraction and dilation of the iris, in order to regulate the intensity of light entering the eye. This is known as the pupillary reflex.
Adler	Adler argued that human personality could be explained teleologically, separate strands dominated by the guiding purpose of the individual's unconscious self ideal to convert feelings of inferiority to superiority (or rather completeness). The desires of the self ideal were countered by social and ethical demands.
Jung	Jung was in some aspects a response to Sigmund Freud's psychoanalysis. He proposed and developed the concepts of the extroverted and introverted personality, archetypes, and the collective unconscious. His work has been influential in psychiatry and in the study of religion, literature, and related fields.
Puberty	Puberty refers to the process of physical changes by which a child's body becomes an adult

Chapter 2. Sigmund Freud

Chapter 2. Sigmund Freud

	body capable of reproduction.
Pleasure principle	The pleasure principle is the tendency to seek pleasure and avoid pain. In Freud's theory, this principle rules the Id, but is at least partly repressed by the reality principle.
Reflection	Reflection is the process of rephrasing or repeating thoughts and feelings expressed, making the person more aware of what they are saying or thinking.
Learning	Learning is a relatively permanent change in behavior that results from experience. Thus, to attribute a behavioral change to learning, the change must be relatively permanent and must result from experience.
Defense mechanism	A Defense mechanism is a set of unconscious ways to protect one's personality from unpleasant thoughts and realities which may otherwise cause anxiety. The notion is an integral part of the psychoanalytic theory.

Chapter 3. Carl Jung

Jung	Jung was in some aspects a response to Sigmund Freud's psychoanalysis. He proposed and developed the concepts of the extroverted and introverted personality, archetypes, and the collective unconscious. His work has been influential in psychiatry and in the study of religion, literature, and related fields.
Personality	Personality refers to the pattern of enduring characteristics that differentiates a person, the patterns of behaviors that make each individual unique.
Unconscious mind	The unconscious mind refers to information processing and brain functioning of which a person is unaware. In Freudian theory, it is the repository of unacceptable thoughts and feelings.
Ego	In Freud's view the Ego serves to balance our primitive needs and our moral beliefs and taboos. Relying on experience, a healthy Ego provides the ability to adapt to reality and interact with the outside world.
Psyche	Psyche is the soul, spirit, or mind as distinguished from the body. In psychoanalytic theory, it is the totality of the id, ego, and superego, including both conscious and unconscious components.
Psychopathology	Psychopathology refers to the field concerned with the nature and development of mental disorders.
Parapsychology	Parapsychology is the study of the evidence involving phenomena where a person seems to affect or to gain information about something through a means not currently explainable within the framework of mainstream, conventional science.
Schizophrenia	Schizophrenia is characterized by persistent defects in the perception or expression of reality. A person suffering from untreated schizophrenia typically demonstrates grossly disorganized thinking, and may also experience delusions or auditory hallucinations
Bleuler	Bleuler is particularly notable for naming schizophrenia, a disorder which was previously known as dementia praecox. Bleuler realised the condition was neither a dementia, nor did it always occur in young people (praecox meaning early) and so gave the condition the name from the Greek for split (schizo) and mind (phrene).
Psychoanalysis	Psychoanalysis refers to the school of psychology that emphasizes the importance of unconscious motives and conflicts as determinants of human behavior. It was Freud's method of exploring human personality.
Hypnosis	Hypnosis is a psychological state whose existence and effects are strongly debated. Some believe that it is a state under which the subject's mind becomes so suggestible that the hypnotist, the one who induces the state, can establish communication with the subconscious mind of the subject and command behavior that the subject would not choose to perform in a conscious state.
Friendship	The essentials of friendship are reciprocity and commitment between individuals who see themselves more or less as equals. Interaction between friends rests on a more equal power base than the interaction between children and adults.
The Interpretation of Dreams	The Interpretation of Dreams is a book by Sigmund Freud. The book introduces the Id, the Ego, and the Superego, and describes Freud's theory of the unconscious with respect to Dream interpretation. Widely considered to be his most important contribution to Psychology.
Dementia praecox	An older term for schizophrenia, chosen to describe what was believed to be an incurable and progressive deterioration of mental functioning beginning in adolescence is called dementia praecox.
Repression	A defense mechanism, repression involves moving thoughts unacceptable to the ego into the unconscious, where they cannot be easily accessed.

Go to **Cram101.com** for the Practice Tests for this Chapter.

Chapter 3. Carl Jung

Chapter 3. Carl Jung

Psychoanalytic	Freud's theory that unconscious forces act as determinants of personality is called psychoanalytic theory. The theory is a developmental theory characterized by critical stages of development.
Ernest Jones	Ernest Jones was arguably the best-known follower of Freud. His writings on the subject of psychoanalysis prompted him to launch The International Journal of Psychoanalysis in 1920.
Sigmund Freud	Sigmund Freud was the founder of the psychoanalytic school, based on his theory that unconscious motives control much behavior, that particular kinds of unconscious thoughts and memories are the source of neurosis, and that neurosis could be treated through bringing these unconscious thoughts and memories to consciousness in psychoanalytic treatment.
Stanley Hall	His laboratory at Johns Hopkins is considered to be the first American laboratory of psychology. In 1887 Stanley Hall founded the American Journal of Psychology. His interests centered around child development and evolutionary theory
Motivation	In psychology, motivation is the driving force (desire) behind all actions of an organism.
Libido	Sigmund Freud suggested that libido is the instinctual energy or force that can come into conflict with the conventions of civilized behavior. Jung, condidered the libido as the free creative, or psychic, energy an individual has to put toward personal development, or individuation.
Motives	Needs or desires that energize and direct behavior toward a goal are motives.
Psychosomatic	A psychosomatic illness is one with physical manifestations and perhaps a supposed psychological cause. It is often diagnosed when any known or identifiable physical cause was excluded by medical examination.
Depression	In everyday language depression refers to any downturn in mood, which may be relatively transitory and perhaps due to something trivial. This is differentiated from Clinical depression which is marked by symptoms that last two weeks or more and are so severe that they interfere with daily living.
Psychosis	Psychosis is a generic term for mental states in which the components of rational thought and perception are severely impaired. Persons experiencing a psychosis may experience hallucinations, hold paranoid or delusional beliefs, demonstrate personality changes and exhibit disorganized thinking. This is usually accompanied by features such as a lack of insight into the unusual or bizarre nature of their behavior, difficulties with social interaction and impairments in carrying out the activities of daily living.
Neurosis	Neurosis, any mental disorder that, although may cause distress, does not interfere with rational thought or the persons' ability to function.
Society	The social sciences use the term society to mean a group of people that form a semi-closed (or semi-open) social system, in which most interactions are with other individuals belonging to the group.
Analytical psychology	Analytical psychology is based upon the movement started by Carl Jung and his followers as distinct from Freudian psychoanalysis. Its aim is the personal experience of the deep forces and motivations underlying human behavior.
Conservation of Energy	The principle of conservation of energy states that the total inflow of energy into a system must equal the total outflow of energy from the system, plus the change in the energy contained within the system. In other words, energy can be converted from one form to another, but it cannot be created or destroyed.
Introversion	A personality trait characterized by intense imagination and a tendency to inhibit impulses is called introversion.

Chapter 3. Carl Jung

Chapter 3. Carl Jung

Extroversion	Extroversion refers to the tendency to be outgoing, adaptable, and sociable.
Regression	Return to a form of behavior characteristic of an earlier stage of development is called regression.
Teleology	While science investigates natural laws and phenomena, Philosophical naturalism and teleology investigate the existence or non-existence of an organizing principle behind those natural laws and phenomena. Philosophical naturalism asserts that there are no such principles. Teleology asserts that there are.
Personal unconscious	The personal unconscious in Jung's theory is the layer of the unconscious containing all of the thoughts and experiences that are accessible to the conscious, as well as the repressed memories and impulses.
Stimulus	A change in an environmental condition that elicits a response is a stimulus.
Collective unconscious	Collective unconscious is a term of analytical psychology, originally coined by Carl Jung. It refers to that part of a person's unconscious which is common to all human beings. It contains archetypes, which are forms or symbols that are manifested by all people in all cultures.
Predisposition	Predisposition refers to an inclination or diathesis to respond in a certain way, either inborn or acquired. In abnormal psychology, it is a factor that lowers the ability to withstand stress and inclines the individual toward pathology.
Archetype	The archetype is a concept of psychologist Carl Jung. They are innate prototypes for ideas, which may subsequently become involved in the interpretation of observed phenomena. A group of memories and interpretations closely associated with an archetype is called a complex.
Apparent movement	Apparent movement is the perceived motion of an object when all that has been presented to the eyes is one or a series of stills.
Nightmare	Nightmare was the original term for the state later known as waking dream, and more currently as sleep paralysis, associated with rapid eye movement (REM) periods of sleep.
Consciousness	The awareness of the sensations, thoughts, and feelings being experienced at a given moment is called consciousness.
Hallucination	A hallucination is a sensory perception experienced in the absence of an external stimulus, as distinct from an illusion, which is a misperception of an external stimulus. They may occur in any sensory modality - visual, auditory, olfactory, gustatory, tactile, or mixed.
Persona	In Jungian archetypal psychology, the Persona is the mask or appearance one presents to the world. It may appear in dreams under various guises.
Anima	Anima, according to Carl Jung, is the feminine side of a man's personal unconscious. It can be identified as all the unconscious feminine psychological qualities that a man possesses.
Social role	Social role refers to expected behavior patterns associated with particular social positions.
Punishment	Punishment is the addtion of a stimulus that reduces the frequency of a response, or the removal of a stimulus that results in a reduction of the response.
Phobia	A persistent, irrational fear of an object, situation, or activity that the person feels compelled to avoid is referred to as a phobia.
Affect	A subjective feeling or emotional tone often accompanied by bodily expressions noticeable to others is called affect.
Altruism	Altruism is being helpful to other people with little or no interest in being rewarded for one's efforts. This is distinct from merely helping others.

Go to Cram101.com for the Practice Tests for this Chapter.

Chapter 3. Carl Jung

Chapter 3. Carl Jung

Intuition	Quick, impulsive thought that does not make use of formal logic or clear reasoning is referred to as intuition.
Trait	An enduring personality characteristic that tends to lead to certain behaviors is called a trait. The term trait also means a genetically inherited feature of an organism.
Creativity	Creativity is the ability to think about something in novel and unusual ways and come up with unique solutions to problems. It involves divergent thinking, having many solutions or views to a problem.
Femininity	Femininity is the set of characteristics defined by a culture for idealized females.
Instinct	Instinct is the word used to describe inherent dispositions towards particular actions. They are generally an inherited pattern of responses or reactions to certain kinds of situations.
Psychotherapy	Psychotherapy is a set of techniques based on psychological principles intended to improve mental health, emotional or behavioral issues.
Projection	Attributing one's own undesirable thoughts, impulses, traits, or behaviors to others is referred to as projection.
Attitude	An enduring mental representation of a person, place, or thing that evokes an emotional response and related behavior is called attitude.
Introvert	Introvert refers to a person whose attention is focused inward; a shy, reserved, timid person.
Extrovert	Extrovert refers to a person whose attention is directed outward; a bold, outgoing person.
Adler	Adler argued that human personality could be explained teleologically, separate strands dominated by the guiding purpose of the individual's unconscious self ideal to convert feelings of inferiority to superiority (or rather completeness). The desires of the self ideal were countered by social and ethical demands.
Logical thought	Drawing conclusions on the basis of formal principles of reasoning is referred to as logical thought.
Subjective experience	Subjective experience refers to reality as it is perceived and interpreted, not as it exists objectively.
Insight	Insight refers to a sudden awareness of the relationships among various elements that had previously appeared to be independent of one another.
Stages	Stages represent relatively discrete periods of time in which functioning is qualitatively different from functioning at other periods.
Maturation	The orderly unfolding of traits, as regulated by the genetic code is called maturation.
Adolescence	The period of life bounded by puberty and the assumption of adult responsibilities is adolescence.
Learning	Learning is a relatively permanent change in behavior that results from experience. Thus, to attribute a behavioral change to learning, the change must be relatively permanent and must result from experience.
Wisdom	Wisdom is the ability to make correct judgments and decisions. It is an intangible quality gained through experience. Whether or not something is wise is determined in a pragmatic sense by its popularity, how long it has been around, and its ability to predict against future events.
Rationalism	Rationalism is a philosophical doctrine that asserts that the truth should be determined by reason and factual analysis, rather than faith, dogma or religious teaching. Rationalism has

Chapter 3. Carl Jung

some similarities in ideology and intent to humanism and atheism, in that it aims to provide a framework for social and philosophical discourse outside of religious or supernatural beliefs.

Dissociation — Dissociation is a psychological state or condition in which certain thoughts, emotions, sensations, or memories are separated from the rest.

Synchronicity — Jung's concept of synchronicity describes the alignment of universal forces with the life experiences of an individual. Jung believed that many experiences perceived as coincidences were not merely due to chance, but instead reflected the creation of an event or circumstance by the alignment of such forces.

Acquisition — Acquisition is the process of adapting to the environment, learning or becoming conditioned. In classical conditoning terms, it is the initial learning of the stimulus response link, which involves a neutral stimulus being associated with a unconditioned stimulus and becoming a conditioned stimulus.

Asylums — Asylums are hospitals specializing in the treatment of persons with mental illness. Psychiatric wards differ only in that they are a unit of a larger hospital.

Human nature — Human nature is the fundamental nature and substance of humans, as well as the range of human behavior that is believed to be invariant over long periods of time and across very different cultural contexts.

Empirical — Empirical means the use of working hypotheses which are capable of being disproved using observation or experiment.

Myers-Briggs — The Myers-Briggs Type Indicator is a psychological test designed to assist a person in identifying their personality preferences. It follows from the theories of Carl Jung. The types tested for, known as dichotomies, are extraversion, introversion, sensing, intuition, thinking, feeling, judging and perceiving.

Introversion and extroversion — Introversion and extroversion refer to "attitudes" and show how a person orients and receives their energy. In the extroverted attitude the energy flow is outward, and the preferred focus is on people and things, whereas in the introverted attitude the energy flow is inward, and the preferred focus is on thoughts and ideas.

Personality type — A persistent style of complex behaviors defined by a group of related traits is referred to as a personality type. Myer Friedman and his co-workers first defined personality types in the 1950s. Friedman classified people into 2 categories, Type A and Type B.

Scientific method — Psychologists gather data in order to describe, understand, predict, and control behavior. Scientific method refers to an approach that can be used to discover accurate information. It includes these steps: understand the problem, collect data, draw conclusions, and revise research conclusions.

Innate — Innate behavior is not learned or influenced by the environment, rather, it is present or predisposed at birth.

Dream analysis — Dream analysis is a part of psychoanalysis that intends to look beneath the manifest content of a dream, i.e., what we perceive in the dream, to the latent content of a dream, i.e., the meaning of the dream and the reason we dreamt it.

American Psychological Association — The American Psychological Association is a professional organization representing psychology in the US. The mission statement is to "advance psychology as a science and profession and as a means of promoting health, education , and human welfare".

Attention — Attention is the cognitive process of selectively concentrating on one thing while ignoring other things. Psychologists have labeled three types of attention: sustained attention, selective attention, and divided attention.

Sympathetic	The sympathetic nervous system activates what is often termed the "fight or flight response". It is an automatic regulation system, that is, one that operates without the intervention of conscious thought.
Reflection	Reflection is the process of rephrasing or repeating thoughts and feelings expressed, making the person more aware of what they are saying or thinking.
Evolution	Commonly used to refer to gradual change, evolution is the change in the frequency of alleles within a population from one generation to the next. This change may be caused by different mechanisms, including natural selection, genetic drift, or changes in population (gene flow).

Chapter 3. Carl Jung

Chapter 4. Alfred Adler

Adler	Adler argued that human personality could be explained teleologically, separate strands dominated by the guiding purpose of the individual's unconscious self ideal to convert feelings of inferiority to superiority (or rather completeness). The desires of the self ideal were countered by social and ethical demands.
Trait	An enduring personality characteristic that tends to lead to certain behaviors is called a trait. The term trait also means a genetically inherited feature of an organism.
Personality	Personality refers to the pattern of enduring characteristics that differentiates a person, the patterns of behaviors that make each individual unique.
The Interpretation of Dreams	The Interpretation of Dreams is a book by Sigmund Freud. The book introduces the Id, the Ego, and the Superego, and describes Freud's theory of the unconscious with respect to Dream interpretation. Widely considered to be his most important contribution to Psychology.
Psychoanalytic	Freud's theory that unconscious forces act as determinants of personality is called psychoanalytic theory. The theory is a developmental theory characterized by critical stages of development.
Society	The social sciences use the term society to mean a group of people that form a semi-closed (or semi-open) social system, in which most interactions are with other individuals belonging to the group.
Infantile sexuality	Freud's insistence that sexuality does not begin with adolescence, that babies are sexual too, is referred to as infantile sexuality.
Psychoanalysis	Psychoanalysis refers to the school of psychology that emphasizes the importance of unconscious motives and conflicts as determinants of human behavior. It was Freud's method of exploring human personality.
Repression	A defense mechanism, repression involves moving thoughts unacceptable to the ego into the unconscious, where they cannot be easily accessed.
Individual psychology	Alfred Adler's individual psychology approach views people as motivated by purposes and goals, being creators of their own lives.
Psychiatrist	A psychiatrist is a physician who specializes in the diagnosis and treatment of psychological disorders.
Counselor	A counselor is a mental health professional who specializes in helping people with problems not involving serious mental disorders.
Existentialism	The view that people are completely free and responsible for their own behavior is existentialism.
Jung	Jung was in some aspects a response to Sigmund Freud's psychoanalysis. He proposed and developed the concepts of the extroverted and introverted personality, archetypes, and the collective unconscious. His work has been influential in psychiatry and in the study of religion, literature, and related fields.
Compensation	In personaility, compensation, according to Adler, is an effort to overcome imagined or real inferiorities by developing one's abilities.
Evolution	Commonly used to refer to gradual change, evolution is the change in the frequency of alleles within a population from one generation to the next. This change may be caused by different mechanisms, including natural selection, genetic drift, or changes in population (gene flow).
Masculinity	Masculinity is a culturally determined value reflecting the set of characteristics of maleness.
Obedience	Obedience is the willingness to follow the will of others. Humans have been shown to be

Go to **Cram101.com** for the Practice Tests for this Chapter.

Chapter 4. Alfred Adler

Chapter 4. Alfred Adler

	surprisingly obedient in the presence of perceived legitimate authority figures, as demonstrated by the Milgram experiment in the 1960s.
Bisexuality	Bisexuality is a sexual orientation characterized by aesthetic attraction, romantic love and sexual desire for both males and females.
Femininity	Femininity is the set of characteristics defined by a culture for idealized females.
Stimulus	A change in an environmental condition that elicits a response is a stimulus.
Neurosis	Neurosis, any mental disorder that, although may cause distress, does not interfere with rational thought or the persons' ability to function.
Striving for superiority	According to Adler, the universal drive to adapt, improve oneself, and master life's challenges is referred to as striving for superiority.
Innate	Innate behavior is not learned or influenced by the environment, rather, it is present or predisposed at birth.
Pleasure principle	The pleasure principle is the tendency to seek pleasure and avoid pain. In Freud's theory, this principle rules the Id, but is at least partly repressed by the reality principle.
Premise	A premise is a statement presumed true within the context of a discourse, especially of a logical argument.
Vaihinger	Vaihinger argued that human beings can never really know the underlying reality of the world, and that as a result we construct systems of thought and then assume that these match reality.
Sensation	Sensation is the first stage in the chain of biochemical and neurologic events that begins with the impinging of a stimulus upon the receptor cells of a sensory organ, which then leads to perception, the mental state that is reflected in statements like "I see a uniformly blue wall."
Theories	Theories are logically self-consistent models or frameworks describing the behavior of a certain natural or social phenomenon. They are broad explanations and predictions concerning phenomena of interest.
Psyche	Psyche is the soul, spirit, or mind as distinguished from the body. In psychoanalytic theory, it is the totality of the id, ego, and superego, including both conscious and unconscious components.
Generalization	In conditioning, the tendency for a conditioned response to be evoked by stimuli that are similar to the stimulus to which the response was conditioned is a generalization. The greater the similarity among the stimuli, the greater the probability of generalization.
Perception	Perception is the process of acquiring, interpreting, selecting, and organizing sensory information.
World-view	World-view is a term calqued from the German word Weltanschauung meaning a look onto the world. It refers to the framework through which an individual interprets the world and interacts in it.
Friendship	The essentials of friendship are reciprocity and commitment between individuals who see themselves more or less as equals. Interaction between friends rests on a more equal power base than the interaction between children and adults.
Attitude	An enduring mental representation of a person, place, or thing that evokes an emotional response and related behavior is called attitude.
Oedipus complex	The Oedipus complex is a concept developed by Sigmund Freud to explain the maturation of the infant boy through identification with the father and desire for the mother.

Go to **Cram101.com** for the Practice Tests for this Chapter.

Chapter 4. Alfred Adler

Chapter 4. Alfred Adler

Creative self	According to Alfred Adler, the self-aware aspect of personality that strives to achieve its full potential is referred to as the creative self.
Heredity	Heredity is the transfer of characteristics from parent to offspring through their genes.
Self-esteem	Self-esteem refers to a person's subjective appraisal of himself or herself as intrinsically positive or negative to some degree.
Illusion	An illusion is a distortion of a sensory perception.
Attention	Attention is the cognitive process of selectively concentrating on one thing while ignoring other things. Psychologists have labeled three types of attention: sustained attention, selective attention, and divided attention.
Anxiety	Anxiety is a complex combination of the feeling of fear, apprehension and worry often accompanied by physical sensations such as palpitations, chest pain and/or shortness of breath.
Masturbation	Masturbation is the manual excitation of the sexual organs, most often to the point of orgasm. It can refer to excitation either by oneself or by another, but commonly refers to such activities performed alone.
Insomnia	Insomnia is a sleep disorder characterized by an inability to sleep and/or to remain asleep for a reasonable period during the night.
Compulsion	An apparently irresistible urge to repeat an act or engage in ritualistic behavior such as hand washing is referred to as a compulsion.
Inferiority complex	An inferiority complex is a feeling that one is inferior to others in some way. It is often unconscious, and is thought to drive afflicted individuals to overcompensate, resulting either in spectacular achievement or extreme antisocial behavior.
Authoritarian	The term authoritarian is used to describe a style that enforces strong and sometimes oppressive measures against those in its sphere of influence, generally without attempts at gaining their consent.
Punishment	Punishment is the addtion of a stimulus that reduces the frequency of a response, or the removal of a stimulus that results in a reduction of the response.
Psychotherapy	Psychotherapy is a set of techniques based on psychological principles intended to improve mental health, emotional or behavioral issues.
Learning	Learning is a relatively permanent change in behavior that results from experience. Thus, to attribute a behavioral change to learning, the change must be relatively permanent and must result from experience.
Emotion	An emotion is a mental states that arise spontaneously, rather than through conscious effort. They are often accompanied by physiological changes.
Self-hypnosis	Self-hypnosis is a process by which an individual trains the subconscious mind to believe something, or systematically schematizes the person's own mental associations, usually for a given purpose. This is accomplished through repetitive, constant self-affirmations, and may be seen as a form of self-induced brainwashing.
Zajonc	Zajonc is best known for his decades of work on the mere exposure effect, the phenomenon that repeated exposure to a stimulus brings about an attitude change in relation to the stimulus.
Variable	A variable refers to a measurable factor, characteristic, or attribute of an individual or a system.
Darwin	Darwin achieved lasting fame as originator of the theory of evolution through natural selection. His book Expression of Emotions in Man and Animals is generally considered the

Chapter 4. Alfred Adler

Chapter 4. Alfred Adler

	first text on comparative psychology.
Socioeconomic	Socioeconomic pertains to the study of the social and economic impacts of any product or service offering, market intervention or other activity on an economy as a whole and on the companies, organization and individuals who are its main economic actors.
Social class	Social class describes the relationships between people in hierarchical societies or cultures. Those with more power usually subordinate those with less power.
Population	Population refers to all members of a well-defined group of organisms, events, or things.
Openness to Experience	Openness to Experience, one of the big-five traits, describes a dimension of cognitive style that distinguishes imaginative, creative people from down-to-earth, conventional people.
Transfer of training	The concept of transfer of training states that knowledge or abilities acquired in one area aids the acquisition of knowledge or abilities in other areas. When prior learning is helpful, it is called positive transfer. When prior learning inhibits new learning, it is called negative transfer.
Questionnaire	A self-report method of data collection or clinical assessment method in which the individual being studied checks off items on a printed list, answers multiple-choice questions, or writes out answers to essay questions aimed at producing a selfdescription is called questionnaire.
Alcoholic	An alcoholic is dependent on alcohol as characterized by craving, loss of control, physical dependence and withdrawal symptoms, and tolerance.
Family therapy	Family therapy is a branch of psychotherapy that treats family problems. Family therapists consider the family as a system of interacting members; as such, the problems in the family are seen to arise as an emergent property of the interactions in the system, rather than ascribed exclusively to the "faults" or psychological problems of individual members.
Group therapy	Group therapy is a form of psychotherapy during which one or several therapists treat a small group of clients together as a group. This may be more cost effective than individual therapy, and possibly even more effective.
Ego psychology	Ego psychology was derived from psychoanalysis. The theory emphasizes the role of the ego in development and attributes psychological disorders to failure of the ego to manage impulses and internal conflicts.
Instinct	Instinct is the word used to describe inherent dispositions towards particular actions. They are generally an inherited pattern of responses or reactions to certain kinds of situations.
Free will	The idea that human beings are capable of freely making choices or decisions is free will.
Humanism	Humanism refers to the philosophy and school of psychology that asserts that people are conscious, self-aware, and capable of free choice, self-fulfillment, and ethical behavior.
Research method	The scope of the research method is to produce some new knowledge. This, in principle, can take three main forms: Exploratory research; Constructive research; and Empirical research.
Dream analysis	Dream analysis is a part of psychoanalysis that intends to look beneath the manifest content of a dream, i.e., what we perceive in the dream, to the latent content of a dream, i.e., the meaning of the dream and the reason we dreamt it.
Social motives	Social motives refer to drives acquired through experience and interaction with others.
Motivation	In psychology, motivation is the driving force (desire) behind all actions of an organism.
Temperament	Temperament refers to a basic, innate disposition to change behavior. The activity level is an important dimension of temperament.

Chapter 4. Alfred Adler

Chapter 4. Alfred Adler

Individual differences	Individual differences psychology studies the ways in which individual people differ in their behavior. This is distinguished from other aspects of psychology in that although psychology is ostensibly a study of individuals, modern psychologists invariably study groups.
Guilt	Guilt describes many concepts related to a negative emotion or condition caused by actions which are believed to be, morally wrong. According to Freud, the avoidance of guilt is the basis for moral behavior.

Chapter 4. Alfred Adler

Chapter 5. Karen Horney

Attitude	An enduring mental representation of a person, place, or thing that evokes an emotional response and related behavior is called attitude.
Jung	Jung was in some aspects a response to Sigmund Freud's psychoanalysis. He proposed and developed the concepts of the extroverted and introverted personality, archetypes, and the collective unconscious. His work has been influential in psychiatry and in the study of religion, literature, and related fields.
Stroke	A stroke occurs when the blood supply to a part of the brain is suddenly interrupted by occlusion, by hemorrhage, or other causes
Psychoanalysis	Psychoanalysis refers to the school of psychology that emphasizes the importance of unconscious motives and conflicts as determinants of human behavior. It was Freud's method of exploring human personality.
Psychoanalyst	A psychoanalyst is a specially trained therapist who attempts to treat the individual by uncovering and revealing to the individual otherwise subconscious factors that are contributing to some undesirable behavior.
Compulsion	An apparently irresistible urge to repeat an act or engage in ritualistic behavior such as hand washing is referred to as a compulsion.
Insight	Insight refers to a sudden awareness of the relationships among various elements that had previously appeared to be independent of one another.
Karen Horney	Karen Horney, a neo-Freudian, deviated from orthodox Freudian analysis by emphasizing environmental and cultural, rather than biological, factors in neurosis.
Emotion	An emotion is a mental states that arise spontaneously, rather than through conscious effort. They are often accompanied by physiological changes.
Meningitis	Meningitis is inflammation of the membranes covering the brain and the spinal cord. Although the most common causes are infection (bacterial, viral, fungal or parasitic), chemical agents and even tumor cells may cause meningitis.
Psychoanalytic	Freud's theory that unconscious forces act as determinants of personality is called psychoanalytic theory. The theory is a developmental theory characterized by critical stages of development.
Adler	Adler argued that human personality could be explained teleologically, separate strands dominated by the guiding purpose of the individual's unconscious self ideal to convert feelings of inferiority to superiority (or rather completeness). The desires of the self ideal were countered by social and ethical demands.
Depression	In everyday language depression refers to any downturn in mood, which may be relatively transitory and perhaps due to something trivial. This is differentiated from Clinical depression which is marked by symptoms that last two weeks or more and are so severe that they interfere with daily living.
Superego	Frued's third psychic structure, which functions as a moral guardian and sets forth high standards for behavior is the superego.
Ego	In Freud's view the Ego serves to balance our primitive needs and our moral beliefs and taboos. Relying on experience, a healthy Ego provides the ability to adapt to reality and interact with the outside world.
Personality	Personality refers to the pattern of enduring characteristics that differentiates a person, the patterns of behaviors that make each individual unique.
Basic evil	According to Horney anything that parents do to frustrate the basic needs of their child and thus undermine the child's feeling of security is considered basic evil.

Chapter 5. Karen Horney

Chapter 5. Karen Horney

Anxiety	Anxiety is a complex combination of the feeling of fear, apprehension and worry often accompanied by physical sensations such as palpitations, chest pain and/or shortness of breath.
Stages	Stages represent relatively discrete periods of time in which functioning is qualitatively different from functioning at other periods.
Physiological needs	The easiest kinds of motivation to analyse, at least superficially, are those based upon obvious physiological needs. These include hunger, thirst, and escape from pain.
Basic anxiety	Basic anxiety is a child's insecurity and doubt when a parent is indifferent, unloving, or disparaging. This anxiety, according to Horney, leads the child to a basic hostility toward his or her parents. The child may then become neurotic as an adult.
Hue	A hue refers to the gradation of color within the optical spectrum, or visible spectrum, of light. Hue may also refer to a particular color within this spectrum, as defined by its dominant wavelength, or the central tendency of its combined wavelengths.
Self-assertion	Self-assertion refers to a direct, honest expression of feelings and desires.
Individuality	According to Cooper, individuality consists of two dimensions: self-assertion and separateness.
Self-image	A person's self-image is the mental picture, generally of a kind that is quite resistant to change, that depicts not only details that are potentially available to objective investigation by others, but also items that have been learned by that person about himself or herself.
Illusion	An illusion is a distortion of a sensory perception.
Neurosis	Neurosis, any mental disorder that, although may cause distress, does not interfere with rational thought or the persons' ability to function.
Feedback	Feedback refers to information returned to a person about the effects a response has had.
Projection	Attributing one's own undesirable thoughts, impulses, traits, or behaviors to others is referred to as projection.
Blind spot	In anatomy, the blind spot is the region of the retina where the optic nerve and blood vessels pass through to connect to the back of the eye. Since there are no light receptors there, a part of the field of vision is not perceived.
Anesthesia	Anesthesia is the process of blocking the perception of pain and other sensations. This allows patients to undergo surgery and other procedures without the distress and pain they would otherwise experience.
Sympathetic	The sympathetic nervous system activates what is often termed the "fight or flight response". It is an automatic regulation system, that is, one that operates without the intervention of conscious thought.
Oedipus complex	The Oedipus complex is a concept developed by Sigmund Freud to explain the maturation of the infant boy through identification with the father and desire for the mother.
Incest	Incest refers to sexual relations between close relatives, most often between daughter and father or between brother and sister.
Determinism	Determinism is the philosophical proposition that every event, including human cognition and action, is causally determined by an unbroken chain of prior occurrences.
Penis	The penis is the external male copulatory organ and the external male organ of urination. In humans, the penis is homologous to the female clitoris, as it develops from the same embryonic structure. It is capable of erection for use in copulation.

Chapter 5. Karen Horney

Chapter 5. Karen Horney

Anatomy	Anatomy is the branch of biology that deals with the structure and organization of living things. It can be divided into animal anatomy (zootomy) and plant anatomy (phytonomy). Major branches of anatomy include comparative anatomy, histology, and human anatomy.
Affective	Affective is the way people react emotionally, their ability to feel another living thing's pain or joy.
Validity	The extent to which a test measures what it is intended to measure is called validity.
Prejudice	Prejudice in general, implies coming to a judgment on the subject before learning where the preponderance of the evidence actually lies, or formation of a judgement without direct experience.
Psychotherapy	Psychotherapy is a set of techniques based on psychological principles intended to improve mental health, emotional or behavioral issues.
Innate	Innate behavior is not learned or influenced by the environment, rather, it is present or predisposed at birth.
Instinct	Instinct is the word used to describe inherent dispositions towards particular actions. They are generally an inherited pattern of responses or reactions to certain kinds of situations.
Schopenhauer	For Schopenhauer, human will had ontological primacy over the intellect; in other words, desire is understood to be prior to thought, and, in a parallel sense, will is said to be prior to being.
Nietzsche	Nietzsche in his own estimation was a psychologist. His works helped to reinforce not only agnostic trends that followed Enlightenment thinkers, and the evolutionary theory of Charles Darwin, but also the interpretations of human behavior by Sigmund Freud.
Goethe	Goethe argued that laws could not be created by pure rationalism, since geography and history shaped habits and patterns. This stood in sharp contrast to the prevailing Enlightenment view that reason was sufficient to create well-ordered societies and good laws.
Incentive	An incentive is what is expected once a behavior is performed. An incentive acts as a reinforcer.
Transference	Transference is a phenomenon in psychology characterized by unconscious redirection of feelings from one person to another.
Early childhood	Early childhood refers to the developmental period extending from the end of infancy to about 5 or 6 years of age; sometimes called the preschool years.
Motivation	In psychology, motivation is the driving force (desire) behind all actions of an organism.
Free association	In psychoanalysis, the uncensored uttering of all thoughts that come to mind is called free association.
Dream analysis	Dream analysis is a part of psychoanalysis that intends to look beneath the manifest content of a dream, i.e., what we perceive in the dream, to the latent content of a dream, i.e., the meaning of the dream and the reason we dreamt it.
Prognosis	A forecast about the probable course of an illess is referred to as prognosis.
Empirical	Empirical means the use of working hypotheses which are capable of being disproved using observation or experiment.
Defense mechanism	A Defense mechanism is a set of unconscious ways to protect one's personality from unpleasant thoughts and realities which may otherwise cause anxiety. The notion is an integral part of the psychoanalytic theory.
Theories	Theories are logically self-consistent models or frameworks describing the behavior of a

Chapter 5. Karen Horney

	certain natural or social phenomenon. They are broad explanations and predictions concerning phenomena of interest.
Humanistic theories	Humanistic theories focus attention on the whole, unique person, especially on the person's conscious understanding of his or her self and the world.
Maslow	Maslow is mostly noted today for his proposal of a hierarchy of human needs which he often presented as a pyramid. Maslow was an instrumental player in the formation of the humanistic movement, also known as the third force in psychology.
Guilt	Guilt describes many concepts related to a negative emotion or condition caused by actions which are believed to be, morally wrong. According to Freud, the avoidance of guilt is the basis for moral behavior.
Self-understanding	Self-understanding is a child's cognitive representation of the self, the substance and content of the child's self-conceptions.
Evolution	Commonly used to refer to gradual change, evolution is the change in the frequency of alleles within a population from one generation to the next. This change may be caused by different mechanisms, including natural selection, genetic drift, or changes in population (gene flow).
American Psychological Association	The American Psychological Association is a professional organization representing psychology in the US. The mission statement is to "advance psychology as a science and profession and as a means of promoting health, education , and human welfare".

Chapter 5. Karen Horney

Chapter 6. Erik H. Erikson

Psychoanalytic	Freud's theory that unconscious forces act as determinants of personality is called psychoanalytic theory. The theory is a developmental theory characterized by critical stages of development.
Anna Freud	Anna Freud was a pioneer of child psychoanalysis. She popularized the notion that adolescence is a period that includes rapid mood fluctuation with enormous uncertainty about self.
Insight	Insight refers to a sudden awareness of the relationships among various elements that had previously appeared to be independent of one another.
Erik Erikson	Erik Erikson conceived eight stages of development, each confronting the individual with its own psychosocial demands, that continued into old age. Personality development, according to Erikson, takes place through a series of crises that must be overcome and internalized by the individual in preparation for the next developmental stage. Such crisis are not catastrophes but vulnerabilities.
Montessori	As an educational approach, the Montessori method's central focus is on the needs, talents, gifts, and special individuality of each child. Montessori practitioners believe children learn best in their own way at their own pace.
Psychoanalyst	A psychoanalyst is a specially trained therapist who attempts to treat the individual by uncovering and revealing to the individual otherwise subconscious factors that are contributing to some undesirable behavor.
Henry Murray	Henry Murray believed that personality could be better understood by investigating the unconscious mind. He is most famous for the development of the Thematic Apperception Test (TAT), a widely used projective measure of personality.
Personality	Personality refers to the pattern of enduring characteristics that differentiates a person, the patterns of behaviors that make each individual unique.
Variable	A variable refers to a measurable factor, characteristic, or attribute of an individual or a system.
Society	The social sciences use the term society to mean a group of people that form a semi-closed (or semi-open) social system, in which most interactions are with other individuals belonging to the group.
Theories	Theories are logically self-consistent models or frameworks describing the behavior of a certain natural or social phenomenon. They are broad explanations and predictions concerning phenomena of interest.
Thyroid	In anatomy, the thyroid is the largest endocrine gland in the body. The primary function of the thyroid is production of hormones.
Stereotype	A stereotype is considered to be a group concept, held by one social group about another. They are often used in a negative or prejudicial sense and are frequently used to justify certain discriminatory behaviors. This allows powerful social groups to legitimize and protect their dominant position
Attention	Attention is the cognitive process of selectively concentrating on one thing while ignoring other things. Psychologists have labeled three types of attention: sustained attention, selective attention, and divided attention.
Construct	A generalized concept, such as anxiety or gravity, is a construct.
Uterus	The uterus or womb is the major female reproductive organ. The main function of the uterus is to accept a fertilized ovum which becomes implanted into the endometrium, and derives nourishment from blood vessels which develop exclusively for this purpose.
Ovum	Ovum is a female sex cell or gamete.

Chapter 6. Erik H. Erikson

Chapter 6. Erik H. Erikson

Ego psychology	Ego psychology was derived from psychoanalysis. The theory emphasizes the role of the ego in development and attributes psychological disorders to failure of the ego to manage impulses and internal conflicts.
Creativity	Creativity is the ability to think about something in novel and unusual ways and come up with unique solutions to problems. It involves divergent thinking, having many solutions or views to a problem.
Superego	Frued's third psychic structure, which functions as a moral guardian and sets forth high standards for behavior is the superego.
Ego	In Freud's view the Ego serves to balance our primitive needs and our moral beliefs and taboos. Relying on experience, a healthy Ego provides the ability to adapt to reality and interact with the outside world.
Autonomy	Autonomy is the condition of something that does not depend on anything else.
Adler	Adler argued that human personality could be explained teleologically, separate strands dominated by the guiding purpose of the individual's unconscious self ideal to convert feelings of inferiority to superiority (or rather completeness). The desires of the self ideal were countered by social and ethical demands.
Stages	Stages represent relatively discrete periods of time in which functioning is qualitatively different from functioning at other periods.
Psychosexual stages	In Freudian theory each child passes through five psychosexual stages. During each stage, the id focuses on a distinct erogenous zone on the body. Suffering from trauma during any of the first three stages may result in fixation in that stage. Freud related the resolutions of the stages with adult personalities and personality disorders.
Basic trust versus basic mistrust	Erikson's first stage, when infants develop trust or mistrust based on the quality of care, love, and affection provided is called the basic trust versus basic mistrust stage.
Psychosexual development	In psychodynamic theory, the process by which libidinal energy is expressed through different erogenous zones during different stages of development is called psychosexual development.
Infancy	The developmental period that extends from birth to 18 or 24 months is called infancy.
Anxiety	Anxiety is a complex combination of the feeling of fear, apprehension and worry often accompanied by physical sensations such as palpitations, chest pain and/or shortness of breath.
Anal stage	The anal stage in psychology is the term used by Sigmund Freud to describe the development during the second year of life, in which a child's pleasure and conflict centers are in the anal area.
Self-esteem	Self-esteem refers to a person's subjective appraisal of himself or herself as intrinsically positive or negative to some degree.
Punishment	Punishment is the addtion of a stimulus that reduces the frequency of a response, or the removal of a stimulus that results in a reduction of the response.
Initiative versus guilt	Initiative versus guilt is Erikson's third stage of development, which occurs during the preschool years. As preschool children encounter a widening social world, they are challenged more than they were as infants.
Learning	Learning is a relatively permanent change in behavior that results from experience. Thus, to attribute a behavioral change to learning, the change must be relatively permanent and must result from experience.

Chapter 6. Erik H. Erikson

Chapter 6. Erik H. Erikson

Guilt	Guilt describes many concepts related to a negative emotion or condition caused by actions which are believed to be, morally wrong. According to Freud, the avoidance of guilt is the basis for moral behavior.
Industry versus inferiority	Erikson's fourth stage of development, industry versus inferiority, develops in the elementary school years. Initiative brings children into contact with a new experiences. They direct their energy toward mastering knowledge and intellectual skills.
Social skills	Social skills are skills used to interact and communicate with others to assist status in the social structure and other motivations.
Identity versus role confusion	Identity versus role confusion, Erikson's fifth psychosocial stage, shows adolescents needing to establish their own identity and to form values to live by. Failure at this stage can lead to an identity crisis.
Genital stage	The genital stage in psychology is the term used by Sigmund Freud to describe the final stage of human psychosexual development. It is characterized by the expression of libido through intercourse with an adult of the other gender.
Adolescence	The period of life bounded by puberty and the assumption of adult responsibilities is adolescence.
Identity crisis	Erikson coinded the term identity crisis: "...a psychosocial state or condition of disorientation and role confusion occurring especially in adolescents as a result of conflicting internal and external experiences, pressures, and expectations and often producing acute anxiety."
Personal identity	The portion of the self-concept that pertains to the self as a distinct, separate individual is called personal identity.
Ambivalence	The simultaneous holding of strong positive and negative emotional attitudes toward the same situation or person is called ambivalence.
Alcoholism	A disorder that involves long-term, repeated, uncontrolled, compulsive, and excessive use of alcoholic beverages and that impairs the drinker's health and work and social relationships is called alcoholism.
Trait	An enduring personality characteristic that tends to lead to certain behaviors is called a trait. The term trait also means a genetically inherited feature of an organism.
Masculinity	Masculinity is a culturally determined value reflecting the set of characteristics of maleness.
Femininity	Femininity is the set of characteristics defined by a culture for idealized females.
Free choice	Free choice refers to the ability to freely make choices that are not controlled by genetics, learning, or unconscious forces.
Ideology	An ideology can be thought of as a comprehensive vision, as a way of looking at things, as in common sense and several philosophical tendencies, or a set of ideas proposed by the dominant class of a society to all members of this society.
Intimacy versus isolation	The life crisis of young adulthood, which is characterized by the task of developing binding intimate relationships is referred to as Erikson's intimacy versus isolation stage.
Friendship	The essentials of friendship are reciprocity and commitment between individuals who see themselves more or less as equals. Interaction between friends rests on a more equal power base than the interaction between children and adults.
Generativity versus	Generativity versus stagnation is Erikson's term for the crisis of middle adulthood. The individual is characterized by the task of being productive and contributing to younger

Chapter 6. Erik H. Erikson

stagnation	generations.
Generativity	Generativity refers to an adult's concern for and commitment to the well-being of future generations.
Cultural values	The importance and desirability of various objects and activities as defined by people in a given culture are referred to as cultural values.
Ego integrity versus despair	Erikson's term for the crisis of late adulthood, characterized by the task of maintaining one's sense of identity despite physical deterioration is called ego integrity versus despair.
Wisdom	Wisdom is the ability to make correct judgments and decisions. It is an intangible quality gained through experience. Whether or not something is wise is determined in a pragmatic sense by its popularity, how long it has been around, and its ability to predict against future events.
Evolution	Commonly used to refer to gradual change, evolution is the change in the frequency of alleles within a population from one generation to the next. This change may be caused by different mechanisms, including natural selection, genetic drift, or changes in population (gene flow).
Psychotherapy	Psychotherapy is a set of techniques based on psychological principles intended to improve mental health, emotional or behavioral issues.
Premise	A premise is a statement presumed true within the context of a discourse, especially of a logical argument.
Clinician	A health professional authorized to provide services to people suffering from one or more pathologies is a clinician.
Jung	Jung was in some aspects a response to Sigmund Freud's psychoanalysis. He proposed and developed the concepts of the extroverted and introverted personality, archetypes, and the collective unconscious. His work has been influential in psychiatry and in the study of religion, literature, and related fields.
Anatomy	Anatomy is the branch of biology that deals with the structure and organization of living things. It can be divided into animal anatomy (zootomy) and plant anatomy (phytonomy). Major branches of anatomy include comparative anatomy, histology, and human anatomy.
Attitude	An enduring mental representation of a person, place, or thing that evokes an emotional response and related behavior is called attitude.
Penis	The penis is the external male copulatory organ and the external male organ of urination. In humans, the penis is homologous to the female clitoris, as it develops from the same embryonic structure. It is capable of erection for use in copulation.
Unconscious mind	The unconscious mind refers to information processing and brain functioning of which a person is unaware. In Freudian theory, it is the repository of unacceptable thoughts and feelings.
Dream analysis	Dream analysis is a part of psychoanalysis that intends to look beneath the manifest content of a dream, i.e., what we perceive in the dream, to the latent content of a dream, i.e., the meaning of the dream and the reason we dreamt it.
Dream symbols	Images in dreams whose personal or emotional meanings differ from their literal meanings are called dream symbols.
Free association	In psychoanalysis, the uncensored uttering of all thoughts that come to mind is called free association.
Neurosis	Neurosis, any mental disorder that, although may cause distress, does not interfere with rational thought or the persons' ability to function.

Go to **Cram101.com** for the Practice Tests for this Chapter.

Chapter 6. Erik H. Erikson

Empirical	Empirical means the use of working hypotheses which are capable of being disproved using observation or experiment.
Csikszentmihalyi	Csikszentmihalyi is noted for his work in the study of happiness, creativity, subjective well-being, and fun, but is best known for his having been the architect of the notion of flow: "... people are most happy when they are in a state of flow--a Zen-like state of total oneness...".
Moral reasoning	Moral reasoning involves concepts of justice, whereas social conventional judgments are concepts of social organization.
Peer pressure	Peer pressure comprises a set of group dynamics whereby a group of people in which one feels comfortable may override the sexual personal habits, individual moral inhibitions or idiosyncratic desires to impose a group norm of attitudes or behaviors.
Marcia	Marcia argued that identity could be viewed as a structure of beliefs, abilities and past experiences regarding the self. Identity is a dynamic, not static structure. At least three aspects of the adolescent's development are important in identity formation: must be confident that they have parental support, must have an established sense of industry, and must be able to adopt a self-reflective stance toward the future.
Problem solving	An attempt to find an appropriate way of attaining a goal when the goal is not readily available is called problem solving.
Instinct	Instinct is the word used to describe inherent dispositions towards particular actions. They are generally an inherited pattern of responses or reactions to certain kinds of situations.
Conformity	Conformity is the degree to which members of a group will change their behavior, views and attitudes to fit the views of the group. The group can influence members via unconscious processes or via overt social pressure on individuals.
Heterosexuality	Sexual attraction and behavior directed to the opposite sex is heterosexuality.
Psychosocial development	Erikson's psychosocial development describe eight developmental stages through which a healthily developing human should pass from infancy to late adulthood. In each stage the person confronts, and hopefully masters, new challenges.
Psychohistory	Psychohistory is the study of the psychological motivations of historical events. It combines the insights of psychotherapy with the research methodology of the social sciences to understand the emotional origin of the social and political behavior of groups and nations, past and present.
Life span	Life span refers to the upper boundary of life, the maximum number of years an individual can live. The maximum life span of human beings is about 120 years of age. Females live an average of 6 years longer than males.
Individual differences	Individual differences psychology studies the ways in which individual people differ in their behavior. This is distinguished from other aspects of psychology in that although psychology is ostensibly a study of individuals, modern psychologists invariably study groups.
Autonomy versus shame and doubt	In Erikson's second stage of development, autonomy versus shame and doubt, which occurs in late infancy and toddlerhood, infants begin to discover that their behavior is their own.
Early childhood	Early childhood refers to the developmental period extending from the end of infancy to about 5 or 6 years of age; sometimes called the preschool years.
Psychiatrist	A psychiatrist is a physician who specializes in the diagnosis and treatment of psychological disorders.
Sympathetic	The sympathetic nervous system activates what is often termed the "fight or flight response". It is an automatic regulation system, that is, one that operates without the intervention of

Go to Cram101.com for the Practice Tests for this Chapter.

Chapter 6. Erik H. Erikson

	conscious thought.
Personality trait	According to the Diagnostic and Statistical Manual of the American Psychiatric Association, a personality trait is a "prominent aspect of personality that is exhibited in a wide range of important social and personal contexts. ...".
Innate	Innate behavior is not learned or influenced by the environment, rather, it is present or predisposed at birth.

Chapter 6. Erik H. Erikson

Chapter 7. Gordon Allport

Functional autonomy	By functional autonomy, Allport meant that your motives today are not dependent on the past. He differentiated between perseverative functional autonomy, which refers to habits, and propriate functional autonomy which is more self-directed than habits and includes values.
Personality	Personality refers to the pattern of enduring characteristics that differentiates a person, the patterns of behaviors that make each individual unique.
Temperament	Temperament refers to a basic, innate disposition to change behavior. The activity level is an important dimension of temperament.
Prejudice	Prejudice in general, implies coming to a judgment on the subject before learning where the preponderance of the evidence actually lies, or formation of a judgement without direct experience.
Allport	Allport was a trait theorist. Those traits he believed to predominate a person's personality were called central traits. Traits such that one could be indentifed by the trait, were referred to as cardinal traits. Central traits and cardinal traits are influenced by environmental factors.
Trait	An enduring personality characteristic that tends to lead to certain behaviors is called a trait. The term trait also means a genetically inherited feature of an organism.
Human nature	Human nature is the fundamental nature and substance of humans, as well as the range of human behavior that is believed to be invariant over long periods of time and across very different cultural contexts.
Personal identity	The portion of the self-concept that pertains to the self as a distinct, separate individual is called personal identity.
Phobia	A persistent, irrational fear of an object, situation, or activity that the person feels compelled to avoid is referred to as a phobia.
Personality trait	According to the Diagnostic and Statistical Manual of the American Psychiatric Association, a personality trait is a "prominent aspect of personality that is exhibited in a wide range of important social and personal contexts. ...".
Structuralism	The school of psychology that argues that the mind consists of three basic elements sensations, feelings, and images which combine to form experience is structuralism-- a term coined by Titchener. They were associationists in that they believed that complex ideas were made up of simpler ideas that were combined in accordance with the laws of association.
Authoritarian	The term authoritarian is used to describe a style that enforces strong and sometimes oppressive measures against those in its sphere of influence, generally without attempts at gaining their consent.
Titchener	Titchener attempted to classify the structures of the mind, not unlike the way a chemist breaks down chemicals into their component parts-water into hydrogen and oxygen for example. He conceived of hydrogen and oxygen as structures of a chemical compound, and sensations and thoughts as structures of the mind. This approach became known as structuralism.
Clinical psychologist	A psychologist, usually with a Ph.D, whose training is in the diagnosis, treatment, or research of psychological and behavioral disorders is a clinical psychologist.
Theories	Theories are logically self-consistent models or frameworks describing the behavior of a certain natural or social phenomenon. They are broad explanations and predictions concerning phenomena of interest.
Humanistic psychology	Humanistic psychology refers to the school of psychology that focuses on the uniqueness of human beings and their capacity for choice, growth, and psychological health.
Humanistic	Humanistic refers to any system of thought focused on subjective experience and human

Chapter 7. Gordon Allport

Chapter 7. Gordon Allport

	problems and potentials.
Individuality	According to Cooper, individuality consists of two dimensions: self-assertion and separateness.
Psychoanalysis	Psychoanalysis refers to the school of psychology that emphasizes the importance of unconscious motives and conflicts as determinants of human behavior. It was Freud's method of exploring human personality.
Behaviorism	The school of psychology that defines psychology as the study of observable behavior and studies relationships between stimuli and responses is called behaviorism. Behaviorism relied heavily on animal research and stated the same principles governed the behavior of both nonhumans and humans.
Gestalt psychology	According to Gestalt psychology, people naturally organize their perceptions according to certain patterns. The tendency is to organize perceptions into wholes and to integrate separate stimuli into meaningful patterns.
Unconscious mind	The unconscious mind refers to information processing and brain functioning of which a person is unaware. In Freudian theory, it is the repository of unacceptable thoughts and feelings.
Adaptation	Adaptation is a lowering of sensitivity to a stimulus following prolonged exposure to that stimulus. Behavioral adaptations are special ways a particular organism behaves to survive in its natural habitat.
Moral judgment	Making decisions about which actions are right and which are wrong is a moral judgment.
Variable	A variable refers to a measurable factor, characteristic, or attribute of an individual or a system.
Psychoanalytic	Freud's theory that unconscious forces act as determinants of personality is called psychoanalytic theory. The theory is a developmental theory characterized by critical stages of development.
Motives	Needs or desires that energize and direct behavior toward a goal are motives.
Need for achievement	Need for Achievement is a term introduced by David McClelland into the field of psychology, referring to an individual's desire for significant accomplishment, mastering of skills, control, or high standards.
Psychometric	Psychometric study is concerned with the theory and technique of psychological measurement, which includes the measurement of knowledge, abilities, attitudes, and personality traits. The field is primarily concerned with the study of differences between individuals
Self-awareness	Realization that one's existence and functioning are separate from those of other people and things is called self-awareness.
Learning	Learning is a relatively permanent change in behavior that results from experience. Thus, to attribute a behavioral change to learning, the change must be relatively permanent and must result from experience.
Innate	Innate behavior is not learned or influenced by the environment, rather, it is present or predisposed at birth.
Instinct	Instinct is the word used to describe inherent dispositions towards particular actions. They are generally an inherited pattern of responses or reactions to certain kinds of situations.
Stimulus	A change in an environmental condition that elicits a response is a stimulus.
Extraversion	Extraversion, one of the big-five personailty traits, is marked by pronounced engagement with the external world. They are people who enjoy being with people, are full of energy, and often experience positive emotions.

Chapter 7. Gordon Allport

Chapter 7. Gordon Allport

Anxiety	Anxiety is a complex combination of the feeling of fear, apprehension and worry often accompanied by physical sensations such as palpitations, chest pain and/or shortness of breath.
Habit	A habit is a response that has become completely separated from its eliciting stimulus. Early learning theorists used the term to describe S-R associations, however not all S-R associations become a habit, rather many are extinguished after reinforcement is withdrawn.
Attitude	An enduring mental representation of a person, place, or thing that evokes an emotional response and related behavior is called attitude.
Cognition	The intellectual processes through which information is obtained, transformed, stored, retrieved, and otherwise used is cognition.
Individual traits	Personality traits that define a person's unique individual qualities are called individual traits.
Common traits	Common traits, according to Allport, are personality characteristics that are shared by most members of a particular culture or grouping.
Idiographic	An idiographic investigation studies the characteristics of an individual in depth.
Nomothetic	Nomothetic measures are contrasted to ipsative or idiothetic measures, where nomothetic measures are measures that can be taken directly by an outside observer, such as weight or how many times a particular behavior occurs, and ipsative measures are self-reports such as a rank-ordered list of preferences.
Evolution	Commonly used to refer to gradual change, evolution is the change in the frequency of alleles within a population from one generation to the next. This change may be caused by different mechanisms, including natural selection, genetic drift, or changes in population (gene flow).
Self-identity	The self-identity is the mental and conceptual awareness and persistent regard that sentient beings hold with regard to their own being.
Self-esteem	Self-esteem refers to a person's subjective appraisal of himself or herself as intrinsically positive or negative to some degree.
Adolescence	The period of life bounded by puberty and the assumption of adult responsibilities is adolescence.
Self-image	A person's self-image is the mental picture, generally of a kind that is quite resistant to change, that depicts not only details that are potentially available to objective investigation by others, but also items that have been learned by that person about himself or herself.
Stages	Stages represent relatively discrete periods of time in which functioning is qualitatively different from functioning at other periods.
Internalization	The developmental change from behavior that is externally controlled to behavior that is controlled by internal standards and principles is referred to as internalization.
Punishment	Punishment is the addtion of a stimulus that reduces the frequency of a response, or the removal of a stimulus that results in a reduction of the response.
Guilt	Guilt describes many concepts related to a negative emotion or condition caused by actions which are believed to be, morally wrong. According to Freud, the avoidance of guilt is the basis for moral behavior.
Motivation	In psychology, motivation is the driving force (desire) behind all actions of an organism.
Drive reduction	Drive reduction theories are based on the need-state. Drive activates behavior. Reinforcement occurs whenever drive is reduced, leading to learning of whatever response solves the need.

Go to **Cram101.com** for the Practice Tests for this Chapter.

Chapter 7. Gordon Allport

	Thus the reduction in need serves as reinforcement and produces reinforcement of the response that leads to it.
Adler	Adler argued that human personality could be explained teleologically, separate strands dominated by the guiding purpose of the individual's unconscious self ideal to convert feelings of inferiority to superiority (or rather completeness). The desires of the self ideal were countered by social and ethical demands.
Reinforcement	In operant conditioning, reinforcement is any change in an environment that (a) occurs after the behavior, (b) seems to make that behavior re-occur more often in the future and (c) that reoccurence of behavior must be the result of the change.
Reflex	A simple, involuntary response to a stimulus is referred to as reflex. Reflex actions originate at the spinal cord rather than the brain.
Self-actualizing	Self-actualizing is the need of a human to make the most of their unique abilities.
Maslow	Maslow is mostly noted today for his proposal of a hierarchy of human needs which he often presented as a pyramid. Maslow was an instrumental player in the formation of the humanistic movement, also known as the third force in psychology.
Jung	Jung was in some aspects a response to Sigmund Freud's psychoanalysis. He proposed and developed the concepts of the extroverted and introverted personality, archetypes, and the collective unconscious. His work has been influential in psychiatry and in the study of religion, literature, and related fields.
Schemata	Cognitive categories or frames of reference are called schemata.
Analogy	An analogy is a comparison between two different things, in order to highlight some form of similarity. Analogy is the cognitive process of transferring information from a particular subject to another particular subject.
Egoism	Egoism is the view that we are always motivated by self-interest, even in seeming acts of altruism.
Society	The social sciences use the term society to mean a group of people that form a semi-closed (or semi-open) social system, in which most interactions are with other individuals belonging to the group.
Positive relationship	Statistically, a positive relationship refers to a mathematical relationship in which increases in one measure are matched by increases in the other.
Generalization	In conditioning, the tendency for a conditioned response to be evoked by stimuli that are similar to the stimulus to which the response was conditioned is a generalization. The greater the similarity among the stimuli, the greater the probability of generalization.
Accommodation	Piaget's developmental process of accommodation is the modification of currently held schemes or new schemes so that new information inconsistent with the existing schemes can be integrated and understood.
Perception	Perception is the process of acquiring, interpreting, selecting, and organizing sensory information.
Meditation	Meditation usually refers to a state in which the body is consciously relaxed and the mind is allowed to become calm and focused.
Puberty	Puberty refers to the process of physical changes by which a child's body becomes an adult body capable of reproduction.
Compensation	In personaility, compensation, according to Adler, is an effort to overcome imagined or real inferiorities by developing one's abilities.

Chapter 7. Gordon Allport

Chapter 7. Gordon Allport

Empirical	Empirical means the use of working hypotheses which are capable of being disproved using observation or experiment.
Nonverbal communication	Communication between individuals that does not involve the content of spoken language, but relies instead on an unspoken language of facial expressions, eye contact, and body language is nonverbal communication.
Denial	Denial is a psychological defense mechanism in which a person faced with a fact that is uncomfortable or painful to accept rejects it instead, insisting that it is not true despite what may be overwhelming evidence.
Predisposition	Predisposition refers to an inclination or diathesis to respond in a certain way, either inborn or acquired. In abnormal psychology, it is a factor that lowers the ability to withstand stress and inclines the individual toward pathology.
Mischel	Mischel is known for his cognitive social learning model of personality that focuses on the specific cognitive variables that mediate the manner in which new experiences affect the individual.
Expressive behaviors	Behaviors that express or communicate emotion or personal feelings are expressive behaviors.
Research method	The scope of the research method is to produce some new knowledge. This, in principle, can take three main forms: Exploratory research; Constructive research; and Empirical research.
Superego	Frued's third psychic structure, which functions as a moral guardian and sets forth high standards for behavior is the superego.

Chapter 8. Raymond B. Cattell and Hans J. Eysenck

Personality	Personality refers to the pattern of enduring characteristics that differentiates a person, the patterns of behaviors that make each individual unique.
Theories	Theories are logically self-consistent models or frameworks describing the behavior of a certain natural or social phenomenon. They are broad explanations and predictions concerning phenomena of interest.
Scientific method	Psychologists gather data in order to describe, understand, predict, and control behavior. Scientific method refers to an approach that can be used to discover accurate information. It includes these steps: understand the problem, collect data, draw conclusions, and revise research conclusions.
Trait	An enduring personality characteristic that tends to lead to certain behaviors is called a trait. The term trait also means a genetically inherited feature of an organism.
Psychopathology	Psychopathology refers to the field concerned with the nature and development of mental disorders.
Factor analysis	Factor analysis is a statistical technique that originated in psychometrics. The objective is to explain the most of the variability among a number of observable random variables in terms of a smaller number of unobservable random variables called factors.
Thorndike	Thorndike worked in animal behavior and the learning process leading to the theory of connectionism. Among his most famous contributions were his research on cats escaping from puzzle boxes, and his formulation of the Law of Effect.
Stanley Hall	His laboratory at Johns Hopkins is considered to be the first American laboratory of psychology. In 1887 Stanley Hall founded the American Journal of Psychology. His interests centered around child development and evolutionary theory
Henry Murray	Henry Murray believed that personality could be better understood by investigating the unconscious mind. He is most famous for the development of the Thematic Apperception Test (TAT), a widely used projective measure of personality.
Allport	Allport was a trait theorist. Those traits he believed to predominate a person's personality were called central traits. Traits such that one could be indentifed by the trait, were referred to as cardinal traits. Central traits and cardinal traits are influenced by environmental factors.
Darwin	Darwin achieved lasting fame as originator of the theory of evolution through natural selection. His book Expression of Emotions in Man and Animals is generally considered the first text on comparative psychology.
Individual differences	Individual differences psychology studies the ways in which individual people differ in their behavior. This is distinguished from other aspects of psychology in that although psychology is ostensibly a study of individuals, modern psychologists invariably study groups.
Stages	Stages represent relatively discrete periods of time in which functioning is qualitatively different from functioning at other periods.
Clinical psychologist	A psychologist, usually with a Ph.D, whose training is in the diagnosis, treatment, or research of psychological and behavioral disorders is a clinical psychologist.
Clinical psychology	Clinical psychology is involved in the diagnosis, assessment, and treatment of patients with mental or behavioral disorders, and conducts research in these various areas.
Psychoanalytic	Freud's theory that unconscious forces act as determinants of personality is called psychoanalytic theory. The theory is a developmental theory characterized by critical stages of development.
Psychotherapy	Psychotherapy is a set of techniques based on psychological principles intended to improve

Chapter 8. Raymond B. Cattell and Hans J. Eysenck

Chapter 8. Raymond B. Cattell and Hans J. Eysenck

	mental health, emotional or behavioral issues.
Experimental psychology	Experimental psychology is an approach to psychology that treats it as one of the natural sciences, and therefore assumes that it is susceptible to the experimental method.
Social psychology	Social psychology is the study of the nature and causes of human social behavior, with an emphasis on how people think towards each other and how they relate to each other.
Correlation	A statistical technique for determining the degree of association between two or more variables is referred to as correlation.
Variable	A variable refers to a measurable factor, characteristic, or attribute of an individual or a system.
Correlation coefficient	Correlation coefficient refers to a number from +1.00 to -1.00 that expresses the direction and extent of the relationship between two variables. The closer to 1, the stronger the relationship. The sign, + or -, indicates the direction.
Positive correlation	A relationship between two variables in which both vary in the same direction is called a positive correlation.
Negative correlation	A negative correlation refers to a relationship between two variables in which one variable increases as the other decreases.
Dependent variable	A measure of an assumed effect of an independent variable is called the dependent variable.
Inductive reasoning	A form of reasoning in which we reason from individual cases or particular facts to a general conclusion is referred to as inductive reasoning. The conclusion can be said to follow with a probability rather than certainty.
Hypothesis	A specific statement about behavior or mental processes that is testable through research is a hypothesis.
Self-report inventories	Personality tests that ask individuals to answer a series of questions about their own characteristic behaviors are called self-report inventories.
Attitude	An enduring mental representation of a person, place, or thing that evokes an emotional response and related behavior is called attitude.
Hypothetico-deductive reasoning	In Piaget's theory, the formal operational ability to think hypothetically is referred to as hypothetico-deductive reasoning.
Experimental hypothesis	The experimental hypothesis is what the investigator assumes will happen in a scientific investigation if certain conditions are met or particular variables are manipulated.
Personality trait	According to the Diagnostic and Statistical Manual of the American Psychiatric Association, a personality trait is a "prominent aspect of personality that is exhibited in a wide range of important social and personal contexts. ...".
Idiographic	An idiographic investigation studies the characteristics of an individual in depth.
Nomothetic	Nomothetic measures are contrasted to ipsative or idiothetic measures, where nomothetic measures are measures that can be taken directly by an outside observer, such as weight or how many times a particular behavior occurs, and ipsative measures are self-reports such as a rank-ordered list of preferences.
Baseline	Measure of a particular behavior or process taken before the introduction of the independent variable or treatment is called the baseline.
Surface trait	A surface trait is Cattell's name for observable qualities of personality, such as those used

Chapter 8. Raymond B. Cattell and Hans J. Eysenck

	to describe a friend.
Source traits	Cattell's name for the traits that make up the most basic personality structure and causes of behavior is source traits.
Questionnaire	A self-report method of data collection or clinical assessment method in which the individual being studied checks off items on a printed list, answers multiple-choice questions, or writes out answers to essay questions aimed at producing a selfdescription is called questionnaire.
Heredity	Heredity is the transfer of characteristics from parent to offspring through their genes.
Fluid intelligence	Mental flexibility in the ability to reason abstractly is called fluid intelligence. Fluid intelligence tends to decline around middle adulthood.
Intelligence test	An intelligence test is a standardized means of assessing a person's current mental ability, for example, the Stanford-Binet test and the Wechsler Adult Intelligence Scale.
Crystallized intelligence	One's lifetime of intellectual achievement, as and shown largely through vocabulary and knowledge of world affairs is called crystallized intelligence.
Nature-nurture	Nature-nurture is a shorthand expression for debates about the relative importance of an individual's "nature" versus personal experiences ("nurture") in determining or causing physical and behavioral traits.
Genetics	Genetics is the science of genes, heredity, and the variation of organisms.
Innate	Innate behavior is not learned or influenced by the environment, rather, it is present or predisposed at birth.
Temperament	Temperament refers to a basic, innate disposition to change behavior. The activity level is an important dimension of temperament.
Emotion	An emotion is a mental states that arise spontaneously, rather than through conscious effort. They are often accompanied by physiological changes.
Instinct	Instinct is the word used to describe inherent dispositions towards particular actions. They are generally an inherited pattern of responses or reactions to certain kinds of situations.
Attention	Attention is the cognitive process of selectively concentrating on one thing while ignoring other things. Psychologists have labeled three types of attention: sustained attention, selective attention, and divided attention.
Selective perception	Selective perception may refer to any number of cognitive biases in psychology related to the way expectations affect perception.
Predisposition	Predisposition refers to an inclination or diathesis to respond in a certain way, either inborn or acquired. In abnormal psychology, it is a factor that lowers the ability to withstand stress and inclines the individual toward pathology.
Instrumentality	In expectancy theory, the belief that performance will lead to rewards is called instrumentality.
Super-ego	The Super-ego stands in opposition to the desires of the Id. The Super-ego is based upon the internalization of the world view, norms and mores a child absorbs from parents and the surrounding environment at a young age. As the conscience, it includes our sense of right and wrong, maintaining taboos specific to a child's internalization of parental culture.
Stimulus	A change in an environmental condition that elicits a response is a stimulus.
Motivation	In psychology, motivation is the driving force (desire) behind all actions of an organism.
Jung	Jung was in some aspects a response to Sigmund Freud's psychoanalysis. He proposed and

Chapter 8. Raymond B. Cattell and Hans J. Eysenck

Chapter 8. Raymond B. Cattell and Hans J. Eysenck

	developed the concepts of the extroverted and introverted personality, archetypes, and the collective unconscious. His work has been influential in psychiatry and in the study of religion, literature, and related fields.
Introvert	Introvert refers to a person whose attention is focused inward; a shy, reserved, timid person.
Extrovert	Extrovert refers to a person whose attention is directed outward; a bold, outgoing person.
Psychoticism	Psychoticism is one of the three traits used by the psychologist Hans Eysenck in his P-E-N model of personality. High levels of this trait were believed by Eysenck to be linked to increased vulnerability to psychoses such as schizophrenia.
Neuroticism	Eysenck's use of the term neuroticism (or Emotional Stability) was proposed as the dimension describing individual differences in the predisposition towards neurotic disorder.
Personality inventory	A self-report questionnaire by which an examinee indicates whether statements assessing habitual tendencies apply to him or her is referred to as a personality inventory.
Scheme	According to Piaget, a hypothetical mental structure that permits the classification and organization of new information is called a scheme.
Extraversion	Extraversion, one of the big-five personailty traits, is marked by pronounced engagement with the external world. They are people who enjoy being with people, are full of energy, and often experience positive emotions.
Hippocrates	Hippocrates was an ancient Greek physician, commonly regarded as one of the most outstanding figures in medicine of all time; he has been called "the father of medicine."
Assertiveness	Assertiveness basically means the ability to express your thoughts and feelings in a way that clearly states your needs and keeps the lines of communication open with the other.
Wundt	Wundt, considered the father of experimental psychology, created the first laboratory in psychology in 1879. His methodology was based on introspection and his body of work founded the school of thought called Voluntarism.
Kant	Kant held that all known objects are phenomena of consciousness and not realities of the mind. But, the known object is not a mere bundle of sensations for it includes unsensational characteristics or manifestation of a priori principles. He insisted that the scientist and the philosopher approached nature with certain implicit principles, and Kant saw his task to be that of finding and making explicit these principles.
Personality type	A persistent style of complex behaviors defined by a group of related traits is referred to as a personality type. Myer Friedman and his co-workers first defined personality types in the 1950s. Friedman classified people into 2 categories, Type A and Type B.
Empirical	Empirical means the use of working hypotheses which are capable of being disproved using observation or experiment.
Classical conditioning	Classical conditioning is a simple form of learning in which an organism comes to associate or anticipate events. A neutral stimulus comes to evoke the response usually evoked by a natural or unconditioned stimulus by being paired repeatedly with the unconditioned stimulus.
Pavlov	Pavlov first described the phenomenon now known as classical conditioning in experiments with dogs.
Hull	Hull is best known for the Drive Reduction Theory which postulated that behavior occurs in response to primary drives such as hunger, thirst, sexual interest, etc. When the goal of the drive is attained the drive is reduced. This reduction of drive serves as a reinforcer for learning.

Chapter 8. Raymond B. Cattell and Hans J. Eysenck

Chapter 8. Raymond B. Cattell and Hans J. Eysenck

Conditioned response	A conditioned response is the response to a stimulus that occurs when an animal has learned to associate the stimulus with a certain positive or negative effect.
Learning	Learning is a relatively permanent change in behavior that results from experience. Thus, to attribute a behavioral change to learning, the change must be relatively permanent and must result from experience.
Reactive inhibition	Hull's 8th postulate was "responding causes fatigue, which operates against the elicitation of a conditioned response." This is known as reactive inhibition. Hull also found that if practice continued without drive reduction that the response would go to extinction (the organism would stop responding).
Extinction	In operant extinction, if no reinforcement is delivered after the response, gradually the behavior will no longer occur in the presence of the stimulus. The process is more rapid following continuous reinforcement rather than after partial reinforcement. In Classical Conditioning, repeated presentations of the CS without being followed by the US results in the extinction of the CS.
Empirical evidence	Facts or information based on direct observation or experience are referred to as empirical evidence.
Arousal theory	Hebb proposed that attention was a function of arousal, the first arousal theory. Hebb proposed that all human beings have a need to maintain their arousal levels and that there is an optimal level for performance.
Brain	The brain controls and coordinates most movement, behavior and homeostatic body functions such as heartbeat, blood pressure, fluid balance and body temperature. Functions of the brain are responsible for cognition, emotion, memory, motor learning and other sorts of learning. The brain is primarily made up of two types of cells: glia and neurons.
Monoamine oxidase	Monoamine oxidase is an enzyme that catalyzes the oxidation of monoamines. They are found bound to the outer membrane of mitochondria in most cell types in the body. Because of the vital role that it play in the inactivation of neurotransmitters, dysfunction (too much/too little MAO activity) is thought to be responsible for a number of neurological disorders.
Testosterone	Testosterone is a steroid hormone from the androgen group. It is the principal male sex hormone and the "original" anabolic steroid.
Hormone	A hormone is a chemical messenger from one cell (or group of cells) to another. The best known are those produced by endocrine glands, but they are produced by nearly every organ system. The function of hormones is to serve as a signal to the target cells; the action of the hormone is determined by the pattern of secretion and the signal transduction of the receiving tissue.
Enzyme	An enzyme is a protein that catalyzes, or speeds up, a chemical reaction. Enzymes are essential to sustain life because most chemical reactions in biological cells would occur too slowly, or would lead to different products, without enzymes.
Heritability	Heritability It is that proportion of the observed variation in a particular phenotype within a particular population, that can be attributed to the contribution of genotype. In other words: it measures the extent to which differences between individuals in a population are due their being different genetically.
Phenotype	The phenotype of an individual organism is either its total physical appearance and constitution, or a specific manifestation of a trait, such as size or eye color, that varies between individuals. Phenotype is determined to some extent by genotype, or by the identity of the alleles that an individual carries at one or more positions on the chromosomes.
Genotype	The genotype is the specific genetic makeup of an individual, usually in the form of DNA. It

Chapter 8. Raymond B. Cattell and Hans J. Eysenck

	codes for the phenotype of that individual. Any given gene will usually cause an observable change in an organism, known as the phenotype.
Variance	The degree to which scores differ among individuals in a distribution of scores is the variance.
Fraternal twins	Fraternal twins usually occur when two fertilized eggs are implanted in the uterine wall at the same time. The two eggs form two zygotes, and these twins are therefore also known as dizygotic. Dizygotic twins are no more similar genetically than any siblings.
Identical twins	Identical twins occur when a single egg is fertilized to form one zygote (monozygotic) but the zygote then divides into two separate embryos. The two embryos develop into foetuses sharing the same womb. Monozygotic twins are genetically identical unless there has been a mutation in development, and they are almost always the same gender.
Gene	A gene is an ultramicroscopic area of the chromosome. It is the smallest physical unit of the DNA molecule that carries a piece of hereditary information.
Superego	Frued's third psychic structure, which functions as a moral guardian and sets forth high standards for behavior is the superego.
Ego	In Freud's view the Ego serves to balance our primitive needs and our moral beliefs and taboos. Relying on experience, a healthy Ego provides the ability to adapt to reality and interact with the outside world.
Instrumental conditioning	Operant conditioning, sometimes called instrumental conditioning, was first extensively studied by Thorndike. In instrumental conditioning, the organism must act in a certain way before it is reinforced; that is, reinforcement is contingent on the organism's behavior.
Acquisition	Acquisition is the process of adapting to the environment, learning or becoming conditioned. In classical conditoning terms, it is the initial learning of the stimulus response link, which involves a neutral stimulus being associated with a unconditioned stimulus and becoming a conditioned stimulus.
Infancy	The developmental period that extends from birth to 18 or 24 months is called infancy.
Trait theory	According to trait theory, personality can be broken down into a limited number of traits, which are present in each individual to a greater or lesser degree. This approach is highly compatible with the quantitative psychometric approach to personality testing.
Kagan	The work of Kagan supports the concept of an inborn, biologically based temperamental predisposition to severe anxiety.
Quantitative	A quantitative property is one that exists in a range of magnitudes, and can therefore be measured. Measurements of any particular quantitative property are expressed as as a specific quantity, referred to as a unit, multiplied by a number.
Mental illness	Mental illness is the term formerly used to mean psychological disorder but less preferred because it implies that the causes of the disorder can be found in a medical disease process.
Systematic desensitization	Systematic desensitization refers to Wolpe's behavioral fear-reduction technique in which a hierarchy of fear-evoking stimuli are presented while the person remains relaxed. The fear-evoking stimuli thereby become associated with muscle relaxation.
Maladaptive	In psychology, a behavior or trait is adaptive when it helps an individual adjust and function well within their social environment. A maladaptive behavior or trait is counterproductive to the individual.
Affect	A subjective feeling or emotional tone often accompanied by bodily expressions noticeable to others is called affect.

Chapter 8. Raymond B. Cattell and Hans J. Eysenck

Wolpe	Wolpe is best known for applying classical conditioning principles to the treatment of phobias, called systematic desensitization. Any "neutral" stimulus, simple or complex that happens to make an impact on an individual at about the time that a fear reaction is evoked acquires the ability to evoke fear subsequently. An acquired CS-CR relationship should be extinguishable.
Behavior therapy	Behavior therapy refers to the systematic application of the principles of learning to direct modification of a client's problem behaviors.
Psychoanalysis	Psychoanalysis refers to the school of psychology that emphasizes the importance of unconscious motives and conflicts as determinants of human behavior. It was Freud's method of exploring human personality.
Placebo	Placebo refers to a bogus treatment that has the appearance of being genuine.
Five-factor model	The five-factor model of personality proposes that there are five universal dimensions of personality: Neuroticism, Extraversion, Openness, Conscientiousness, and Agreeableness.
Big five	The big five factors of personality are Openness to experience, Conscientiousness, Extraversion, Agreeableness, and Emotional Stability.
Thurstone	Thurstone was a pioneer in the field of psychometrics. His work in factor analysis led him to formulate a model of intelligence center around "Primary Mental Abilities", which were independent group factors of intelligence that different individuals possessed in varying degrees.
Lexical Hypothesis	Those individual differences that are most salient and socially relevant in people's lives will eventually become encoded into their language; the more important such a difference, the more likely is it to become expressed as a single word. This is the Lexical Hypothesis.
Conscientiousness	Conscientiousness is one of the dimensions of the five-factor model of personality and individual differences involving being organized, thorough, and reliable as opposed to careless, negligent, and unreliable.
Agreeableness	Agreeableness, one of the big-five personality traits, reflects individual differences in concern with cooperation and social harmony. It is the degree individuals value getting along with others.
Extroversion	Extroversion refers to the tendency to be outgoing, adaptable, and sociable.
Simulation	A simulation is an imitation of some real device or state of affairs. Simulation attempts to represent certain features of the behavior of a physical or abstract system by the behavior of another system.
Sensation seeking	A generalized preference for high or low levels of sensory stimulation is referred to as sensation seeking.
Suicide	Suicide behavior is rare in childhood but escalates in adolescence. The suicide rate increases in a linear fashion from adolescence through late adulthood.
Population	Population refers to all members of a well-defined group of organisms, events, or things.
Adolescence	The period of life bounded by puberty and the assumption of adult responsibilities is adolescence.
Threshold	In general, a threshold is a fixed location or value where an abrupt change is observed. In the sensory modalities, it is the minimum amount of stimulus energy necessary to elicit a sensory response.
Conditioning	Conditioning describes the process by which behaviors can be learned or modified through interaction with the environment.

Chapter 8. Raymond B. Cattell and Hans J. Eysenck

Partial reinforcement	In a partial reinforcement environment, not every correct response is reinforced. Partial reinforcement is usually introduced after a continuous reinforcement schedule has acquired the behavior.
Threshold method	The threshold method of breaking a habit involves presenting cues at such low levels that the response does not occur. The stimulus is then increased thus raising the response threshold. Breaking up a habit involves finding the cues that initiate the action and practicing another response to such cues.
Sedative	A sedative is a drug that depresses the central nervous system (CNS), which causes calmness, relaxation, reduction of anxiety, sleepiness, slowed breathing, slurred speech, staggering gait, poor judgment, and slow, uncertain reflexes.
Electroencephalogram	Electroencephalography is the neurophysiologic measurement of the electrical activity of the brain by recording from electrodes placed on the scalp, or in the special cases on the cortex. The resulting traces are known as an electroencephalogram and represent so-called brainwaves.
Socialization	Social rules and social relations are created, communicated, and changed in verbal and nonverbal ways creating social complexity useful in identifying outsiders and intelligent breeding partners. The process of learning these skills is called socialization.
Mischel	Mischel is known for his cognitive social learning model of personality that focuses on the specific cognitive variables that mediate the manner in which new experiences affect the individual.
Reification	Reification is the constructive or generative aspect of perception whereby the experienced percept contains more explicit spatial information than the sensory stimulus on which it is based.
Natural selection	Natural selection is a process by which biological populations are altered over time, as a result of the propagation of heritable traits that affect the capacity of individual organisms to survive and reproduce.
Evolution	Commonly used to refer to gradual change, evolution is the change in the frequency of alleles within a population from one generation to the next. This change may be caused by different mechanisms, including natural selection, genetic drift, or changes in population (gene flow).
Scientific research	Research that is objective, systematic, and testable is called scientific research.
Human nature	Human nature is the fundamental nature and substance of humans, as well as the range of human behavior that is believed to be invariant over long periods of time and across very different cultural contexts.
Personality test	A personality test aims to describe aspects of a person's character that remain stable across situations.
Overt behavior	An action or response that is directly observable and measurable is an overt behavior.
Biological needs	Beyond physiological needs for survival, the next level are motivations that have an obvious biological basis but are not required for the immediate survival of the organism. These biological needs include the powerful motivations for sex, parenting and aggression.
Primary drive	A primary drive is a state of tension or arousal arising from a biological or innate need; it is one not based on learning. A primary drive activates behavior.
Introversion	A personality trait characterized by intense imagination and a tendency to inhibit impulses is called introversion.
Maturation	The orderly unfolding of traits, as regulated by the genetic code is called maturation.

Chapter 8. Raymond B. Cattell and Hans J. Eysenck

Hans Eysenck	Hans Eysenck using Factor Analysis concluded that all human traits can be broken down into two distinct categories: 1. Extroversion-Introversion, 2. Neuroticism. He called these categories Supertraits.
American Psychological Association	The American Psychological Association is a professional organization representing psychology in the US. The mission statement is to "advance psychology as a science and profession and as a means of promoting health, education, and human welfare".
Ascending reticular activating system	Ascending reticular activating system are the afferent fibers running through the reticular formation that influence physiological arousal.
Reticular formation	Reticular formation is a part of the brain which is involved in stereotypical actions, such as walking, sleeping, and lying down. The reticular formation, phylogenetically one of the oldest portions of the brain, is a poorly-differentiated area of the brain stem.
Brain stem	The brain stem is the stalk of the brain below the cerebral hemispheres. It is the major route for communication between the forebrain and the spinal cord and peripheral nerves. It also controls various functions including respiration, regulation of heart rhythms, and primary aspects of sound localization.
Neuron	The neuron is the primary cell of the nervous system. They are found in the brain, the spinal cord, in the nerves and ganglia of the peripheral nervous system. It is a specialized cell that conducts impulses through the nervous system and contains three major parts: cell body, dendrites, and an axon. It can have many dendrites but only one axon.
Anxiety	Anxiety is a complex combination of the feeling of fear, apprehension and worry often accompanied by physical sensations such as palpitations, chest pain and/or shortness of breath.
Variability	Statistically, variability refers to how much the scores in a distribution spread out, away from the mean.
Aversive stimulus	A stimulus that elicits pain, fear, or avoidance is an aversive stimulus.
Self-esteem	Self-esteem refers to a person's subjective appraisal of himself or herself as intrinsically positive or negative to some degree.
Depression	In everyday language depression refers to any downturn in mood, which may be relatively transitory and perhaps due to something trivial. This is differentiated from Clinical depression which is marked by symptoms that last two weeks or more and are so severe that they interfere with daily living.
Shyness	A tendency to avoid others plus uneasiness and strain when socializing is called shyness.
Guilt	Guilt describes many concepts related to a negative emotion or condition caused by actions which are believed to be, morally wrong. According to Freud, the avoidance of guilt is the basis for moral behavior.
Egocentricity	Egocentricity in Piaget's theory is the tendency to interpret objects and events from one's own perspective.
Creativity	Creativity is the ability to think about something in novel and unusual ways and come up with unique solutions to problems. It involves divergent thinking, having many solutions or views to a problem.

Chapter 8. Raymond B. Cattell and Hans J. Eysenck

Chapter 9. B. F. Skinner

Skinner	Skinner conducted research on shaping behavior through positive and negative reinforcement, and demonstrated operant conditioning, a technique which he developed in contrast with classical conditioning.
Adolescence	The period of life bounded by puberty and the assumption of adult responsibilities is adolescence.
Punishment	Punishment is the addtion of a stimulus that reduces the frequency of a response, or the removal of a stimulus that results in a reduction of the response.
Pavlov	Pavlov first described the phenomenon now known as classical conditioning in experiments with dogs.
Identity crisis	Erikson coinded the term identity crisis: "...a psychosocial state or condition of disorientation and role confusion occurring especially in adolescents as a result of conflicting internal and external experiences, pressures, and expectations and often producing acute anxiety."
Habit	A habit is a response that has become completely separated from its eliciting stimulus. Early learning theorists used the term to describe S-R associations, however not all S-R associations become a habit, rather many are extinguished after reinforcement is withdrawn.
Walden Two	Walden Two, a novel by B.F. Skinner, describes a fictional community designed around behavioral principles. The fictional utopian commune thrives on a level of productivity and happiness of its citizens far in advance of that in the outside world due to it's practice of scientific social planning and the use of operant conditioning in the raising of children.
Learning	Learning is a relatively permanent change in behavior that results from experience. Thus, to attribute a behavioral change to learning, the change must be relatively permanent and must result from experience.
Society	The social sciences use the term society to mean a group of people that form a semi-closed (or semi-open) social system, in which most interactions are with other individuals belonging to the group.
Schedules of Reinforcement	Different combinations of frequency and timing of reinforcement following a behavior are referred to as schedules of reinforcement. They are either continuous (the behavior is reinforced each time it occurs) or intermittent (the behavior is reinforced only on certain occasions).
Verbal Behavior	Verbal Behavior is a book written by B.F. Skinner in which the author presents his ideas on language. For Skinner, speech, along with other forms of communication, was simply a behavior. Skinner argued that each act of speech is an inevitable consequence of the speaker's current environment and his behavioral and sensory history.
Beyond Freedom and Dignity	Beyond Freedom and Dignity is a book-length essay written by B. F. Skinner. The book argued that entrenched belief in free will and the moral autonomy of the individual hindered the prospect of building a happier and better organized society through the use of scientific techniques for modifying behavior.
Behaviorism	The school of psychology that defines psychology as the study of observable behavior and studies relationships between stimuli and responses is called behaviorism. Behaviorism relied heavily on animal research and stated the same principles governed the behavior of both nonhumans and humans.
Personality	Personality refers to the pattern of enduring characteristics that differentiates a person, the patterns of behaviors that make each individual unique.
Theories	Theories are logically self-consistent models or frameworks describing the behavior of a certain natural or social phenomenon. They are broad explanations and predictions concerning

Go to **Cram101.com** for the Practice Tests for this Chapter.

Chapter 9. B. F. Skinner

	phenomena of interest.
Trait	An enduring personality characteristic that tends to lead to certain behaviors is called a trait. The term trait also means a genetically inherited feature of an organism.
Anxiety	Anxiety is a complex combination of the feeling of fear, apprehension and worry often accompanied by physical sensations such as palpitations, chest pain and/or shortness of breath.
Overt behavior	An action or response that is directly observable and measurable is an overt behavior.
Consciousness	The awareness of the sensations, thoughts, and feelings being experienced at a given moment is called consciousness.
Basic emotions	Basic emotions are those found in all cultures, as evidinced by the same facial expressions. They include: fear, anger, disgust, surprise, happiness, and distress.
Causation	Causation concerns the time order relationship between two or more objects such that if a specific antecendent condition occurs the same consequent must always follow.
Animism	Animism is the belief that inanimate objects have lifelike qualities, are capable of action, and possibly thought.
Ego psychology	Ego psychology was derived from psychoanalysis. The theory emphasizes the role of the ego in development and attributes psychological disorders to failure of the ego to manage impulses and internal conflicts.
Persona	In Jungian archetypal psychology, the Persona is the mask or appearance one presents to the world. It may appear in dreams under various guises.
Ego	In Freud's view the Ego serves to balance our primitive needs and our moral beliefs and taboos. Relying on experience, a healthy Ego provides the ability to adapt to reality and interact with the outside world.
Hypothesis	A specific statement about behavior or mental processes that is testable through research is a hypothesis.
Deduction	Deduction refers to reasoning from the general to the particular, as in the case of creating an expected hypothesis for a particular experiment from a general theoretical statement.
Empirical	Empirical means the use of working hypotheses which are capable of being disproved using observation or experiment.
Stages	Stages represent relatively discrete periods of time in which functioning is qualitatively different from functioning at other periods.
Functional analysis	A systematic study of behavior in which one identifies the stimuli that trigger the behavior and the reinforcers that maintain it is a functional analysis. Relations between the two become the cause-and-effect relationships in behavior and are the laws of a science. A synthesis of these various laws expressed in quantitative terms yields a comprehensive picture of the organism as a behaving system without postulating internal processes.
Evolutionary theory	Evolutionary theory is concerned with heritable variability rather than behavioral variations. Natural selection requirements: (1) natural variability within a species must exist, (2) only some individual differences are heritable, and (3) natural selection only takes place when there is an interaction between the inborn attributes of organisms and the environment in which they live.
Acquisition	Acquisition is the process of adapting to the environment, learning or becoming conditioned. In classical conditoning terms, it is the initial learning of the stimulus response link, which involves a neutral stimulus being associated with a unconditioned stimulus and becoming

Chapter 9. B. F. Skinner

	a conditioned stimulus.
Natural selection	Natural selection is a process by which biological populations are altered over time, as a result of the propagation of heritable traits that affect the capacity of individual organisms to survive and reproduce.
Evolution	Commonly used to refer to gradual change, evolution is the change in the frequency of alleles within a population from one generation to the next. This change may be caused by different mechanisms, including natural selection, genetic drift, or changes in population (gene flow).
Shaping	The concept of reinforcing successive, increasingly accurate approximations to a target behavior is called shaping. The target behavior is broken down into a hierarchy of elemental steps, each step more sophisticated then the last. By successively reinforcing each of the the elemental steps, a form of differential reinforcement, until that step is learned while extinguishing the step below, the target behavior is gradually achieved.
Operant behavior	Operant behavior is simply emitted by an organism, that is, all organisms are inherently active, emitting responses that operate in the environment. Unlike respondent behavior, which is dependent on the stimulus that preceded it, operant behavior is a function of its consequences.
Unconditioned stimulus	In classical conditioning, an unconditioned stimulus elicits a response from an organism prior to conditioning. It is a naturally occurring stimulus and a naturally occurring response..
Stimulus	A change in an environmental condition that elicits a response is a stimulus.
Unconditioned response	An Unconditioned Response is the response elicited to an unconditioned stimulus. It is a natural, automatic response.
Respondent Behavior	Respondent behavior refers to behavior that is elicited involuntarily as a reaction to a stimulus. Respondent behavior is identical to classical conditioning UC to UR relationships.
Operant Conditioning	A simple form of learning in which an organism learns to engage in behavior because it is reinforced is referred to as operant conditioning. The consequences of a behavior produce changes in the probability of the behavior's occurence.
Psychotherapy	Psychotherapy is a set of techniques based on psychological principles intended to improve mental health, emotional or behavioral issues.
Conditioning	Conditioning describes the process by which behaviors can be learned or modified through interaction with the environment.
Reinforcer	In operant conditioning, a reinforcer is any stimulus that increases the probability that a preceding behavior will occur again. In Classical Conditioning, the unconditioned stimulus (US) is the reinforcer.
Type R	A type R behavior empahsizes the importance of the response and that it is an operant behavior. The strength of the association is indicated by the rate of responding.
Operant Response	An operant response refers to any behavioral response that produces some reliable effect on the environment that influences the likelihood that the individual will produce that response again.
Variable	A variable refers to a measurable factor, characteristic, or attribute of an individual or a system.
Skinner box	An operant conditioning chamber, or Skinner box, is an experimental apparatus used to study conditioning in animals. Chambers have at least one operandum that can automatically detect the occurrence of a behavioral response or action. The other minimal requirement of a conditioning chamber is that it have a means of delivering a primary reinforcer or

Chapter 9. B. F. Skinner

	unconditioned stimulus like food or water.
Extinction	In operant extinction, if no reinforcement is delivered after the response, gradually the behavior will no longer occur in the presence of the stimulus. The process is more rapid following continuous reinforcement rather than after partial reinforcement. In Classical Conditioning, repeated presentations of the CS without being followed by the US results in the extinction of the CS.
Babbling	Babbling is a stage in child language acquisition, during which an infant appears to be experimenting with making the sounds of language, but not yet producing any recognizable words.
Behavior modification	Behavior Modification is a technique of altering an individual's reactions to stimuli through positive reinforcement and the extinction of maladaptive behavior.
Stimulus generalization	When animals are trained to respond to a single stimulus and test stimuli are introduced that differ from the training stimulus, generally along a single dimension, the systematic decrement in responding typically found has been called the gradient of stimulus generalization.
Secondary Reinforcer	A conditioned reinforcer, sometimes called a secondary reinforcer, is a stimulus or situation that has acquired reinforcing power after being paired in the environment with an unconditioned reinforcer or an earlier conditioned reinforcer.
Primary Reinforcer	Any stimulus whose reinforcing effect is immediate and not a function of previous experience is a primary reinforcer (eg, food, water, warmth).
Reinforcement	In operant conditioning, reinforcement is any change in an environment that (a) occurs after the behavior, (b) seems to make that behavior re-occur more often in the future and (c) that reoccurence of behavior must be the result of the change.
Species	Species refers to a reproductively isolated breeding population.
Generalized reinforcer	Generalized reinforcer refers to any secondary reinforcer that has been paired with several different primary reinforcers.
Chaining	Chaining involves reinforcing individual responses occurring in a sequence to form a complex behavior. It is frequently used for training behavioral sequences that are beyond the current repetoire of the learner.
Primary reinforcement	The use of reinforcers that are innately or biologically satisfying is called primary reinforcement.
Creativity	Creativity is the ability to think about something in novel and unusual ways and come up with unique solutions to problems. It involves divergent thinking, having many solutions or views to a problem.
Nativist	A nativist believes that certain skills or abilities are native or hard wired into the brain at birth.
Gene	A gene is an ultramicroscopic area of the chromosome. It is the smallest physical unit of the DNA molecule that carries a piece of hereditary information.
Mand	The mand is verbal behavior whose form is controlled by states of deprivation and aversion; it is often said to "specify its own reinforcer." What this means loosely is that the function of a mand is to request or to obtain what is wanted.
Echoic	In order to learn any skill, a child must have an imitation repertoire. The echoic is the verbal operant that relates to vocal imitation. An echoic is verbal behavior whose form is controlled by someone else's verbal behavior with point-to-point (1:1) correspondence.

Chapter 9. B. F. Skinner

Chapter 9. B. F. Skinner

Chomsky	Chomsky has greatly influenced the field of theoretical linguistics with his work on the theory of generative grammar. Accordingly, humans are biologically prewired to learn language at a certain time and in a certain way.
Brain	The brain controls and coordinates most movement, behavior and homeostatic body functions such as heartbeat, blood pressure, fluid balance and body temperature. Functions of the brain are responsible for cognition, emotion, memory, motor learning and other sorts of learning. The brain is primarily made up of two types of cells: glia and neurons.
Continuous reinforcement	In continuous reinforcement, every response results in reinforcement.
Partial reinforcement	In a partial reinforcement environment, not every correct response is reinforced. Partial reinforcement is usually introduced after a continuous reinforcement schedule has acquired the behavior.
Experimental psychology	Experimental psychology is an approach to psychology that treats it as one of the natural sciences, and therefore assumes that it is susceptible to the experimental method.
Response-contingent	Reinforcement, punishment, or other consequences that are applied only when a certain response is made are response-contingent consequences.
Variable interval	In a variable interval schedule of reinforcement, reinforcement occurs after the passage of a varying length of time around an average, provided that at least one response occurred in that period.
Variable ratio	In a variable ratio schedule of reinforcement, the number of responses required between reinforcements varies, but on average equals a predetermined number. The variable ratio schedule produces both the highest rate of responding and the greatest resistance to extinction.
Resistance to extinction	Resistance to extinction is the phenomenon that occurs when an organism continues to make a response even after the delivery of the reinforcer for the response has been all or partially eliminated.
Schedule of reinforcement	A schedule of reinforcement is either continuous (the behavior is reinforced each time it occurs) or intermittent (the behavior is reinforced only on certain occasions).
Superstitious behavior	"When small amounts of food are repeatedly given, a 'superstitious ritual' may be set up. This is due not only to the fact that a reinforcing stimulus strengthens any behavior it may happen to follow, even though a contingency has not been explicitly arranged, but also to the fact that the change in behavior resulting from one accidental contingency makes similar accidents more probable."-- Skinner on superstitious behavior.
Noncontingent reinforcement	Noncontingent reinforcement refers to the procedure of providing reinforcers independently of behavior.
Reinforcement contingencies	The circumstances or rules that determine whether responses lead to the presentation of reinforcers are referred to as reinforcement contingencies. Skinner defined culture as a set of reinforcement contingencies.
Positive reinforcement	In positive reinforcement, a stimulus is added and the rate of responding increases.
Positive reinforcer	In operant conditioning, a stimulus that is presented after a response that increases the likelihood that the response will be repeated is a positive reinforcer.
Negative Reinforcement	During negative reinforcement, a stimulus is removed and the frequency of the behavior or response increases.
Negative	Negative reinforcer is a reinforcer that when removed increases the frequency of an response.

Chapter 9. B. F. Skinner

Chapter 9. B. F. Skinner

reinforcer	
Neutral stimulus	A stimulus prior to conditioning that does not naturally result in the response of interest is called a neutral stimulus.
Survey	A method of scientific investigation in which a large sample of people answer questions about their attitudes or behavior is referred to as a survey.
Corporal punishment	Corporal punishment is the use of physical force with the intention of causing pain, but not injury.
Nicotine	Nicotine is an organic compound, an alkaloid found naturally throughout the tobacco plant, with a high concentration in the leaves. It is a potent nerve poison and is included in many insecticides. In lower concentrations, the substance is a stimulant and is one of the main factors leading to the pleasure and habit-forming qualities of tobacco smoking.
Behavior therapy	Behavior therapy refers to the systematic application of the principles of learning to direct modification of a client's problem behaviors.
Alcoholism	A disorder that involves long-term, repeated, uncontrolled, compulsive, and excessive use of alcoholic beverages and that impairs the drinker's health and work and social relationships is called alcoholism.
Abnormal behavior	An action, thought, or feeling that is harmful to the person or to others is called abnormal behavior.
Juvenile delinquency	Juvenile delinquency refers to a broad range of child and adolescent behaviors, including socially unacceptable behavior, status offenses, and criminal acts.
Mental retardation	Mental retardation refers to having significantly below-average intellectual functioning and limitations in at least two areas of adaptive functioning. Many categorize retardation as mild, moderate, severe, or profound.
Drug addiction	Drug addiction, or substance dependence is the compulsive use of drugs, to the point where the user has no effective choice but to continue use.
Obesity	The state of being more than 20 percent above the average weight for a person of one's height is called obesity.
Phobia	A persistent, irrational fear of an object, situation, or activity that the person feels compelled to avoid is referred to as a phobia.
Autism	Autism is a neurodevelopmental disorder that manifests itself in markedly abnormal social interaction, communication ability, patterns of interests, and patterns of behavior.
Token economy	An environmental setting that fosters desired behavior by reinforcing it with tokens that can be exchanged for other reinforcers is called a token economy.
Maladaptive	In psychology, a behavior or trait is adaptive when it helps an individual adjust and function well within their social environment. A maladaptive behavior or trait is counterproductive to the individual.
Psychosis	Psychosis is a generic term for mental states in which the components of rational thought and perception are severely impaired. Persons experiencing a psychosis may experience hallucinations, hold paranoid or delusional beliefs, demonstrate personality changes and exhibit disorganized thinking. This is usually accompanied by features such as a lack of insight into the unusual or bizarre nature of their behavior, difficulties with social interaction and impairments in carrying out the activities of daily living.
Contingency management	Providing a supply of reinforcers to promote and maintain desired behaviors, and the prompt removal of reinforcers that maintain undesired behaviors is called contingency management.

Chapter 9. B. F. Skinner

Utopian	An ideal vision of society is a utopian society.
Narcotic	The term narcotic originally referred to a variety of substances that induced sleep (such state is narcosis). In legal context, narcotic refers to opium, opium derivatives, and their semisynthetic or totally synthetic substitutes.
Human nature	Human nature is the fundamental nature and substance of humans, as well as the range of human behavior that is believed to be invariant over long periods of time and across very different cultural contexts.
American Psychological Association	The American Psychological Association is a professional organization representing psychology in the US. The mission statement is to "advance psychology as a science and profession and as a means of promoting health, education, and human welfare".
Applied Behavior Analysis	Applied Behavior Analysis is the application of behavioral science to the analysis of behavior. It is widely regarded as the most researched intervention in addressing the social, linguistic, and mental differences in autistics.
Generalization	In conditioning, the tendency for a conditioned response to be evoked by stimuli that are similar to the stimulus to which the response was conditioned is a generalization. The greater the similarity among the stimuli, the greater the probability of generalization.
Cognitive psychology	Cognitive psychology is the psychological science which studies the mental processes that are hypothesised to underlie behavior. This covers a broad range of research domains, examining questions about the workings of memory, attention, perception, knowledge representation, reasoning, creativity and problem solving.
Determinism	Determinism is the philosophical proposition that every event, including human cognition and action, is causally determined by an unbroken chain of prior occurrences.
Differential reinforcement	Any training procedure in which certain kinds of behavior are systematically reinforced and others are not is called differential reinforcement. Differential reinforcement involves both reinforcement and extinction.
Successive approximations	In operant conditioning, a series of behaviors that gradually become more similar to a target behavior are called successive approximations.
Attention	Attention is the cognitive process of selectively concentrating on one thing while ignoring other things. Psychologists have labeled three types of attention: sustained attention, selective attention, and divided attention.
Radical behaviorism	Skinner defined behavior to include everything that an organism does, including thinking, feeling and speaking and argued that these phenomena were valid subject matters of psychology. The term Radical Behaviorism refers to "everything an organism does is a behavior."
Type S	A Type S emphasizes the importance of the stimulus in eliciting the desired response. A Type S behavior is a respondent behavior and the strength of the association is indicated by the size of the response.
Behavioristic position	The behavioristic position is that a person comes under the control of a stimulating environment, responds to subtle properties of that environment, and responds to it in many complex ways because of the consequences contingent upon earlier responses.
Sympathetic	The sympathetic nervous system activates what is often termed the "fight or flight response". It is an automatic regulation system, that is, one that operates without the intervention of conscious thought.
Reflection	Reflection is the process of rephrasing or repeating thoughts and feelings expressed, making the person more aware of what they are saying or thinking.

Go to **Cram101.com** for the Practice Tests for this Chapter.

Chapter 9. B. F. Skinner

Chapter 9. B. F. Skinner

Humanism	Humanism refers to the philosophy and school of psychology that asserts that people are conscious, self-aware, and capable of free choice, self-fulfillment, and ethical behavior.
Aversive stimulus	A stimulus that elicits pain, fear, or avoidance is an aversive stimulus.
Classical conditioning	Classical conditioning is a simple form of learning in which an organism comes to associate or anticipate events. A neutral stimulus comes to evoke the response usually evoked by a natural or unconditioned stimulus by being paired repeatedly with the unconditioned stimulus.
Conditioned response	A conditioned response is the response to a stimulus that occurs when an animal has learned to associate the stimulus with a certain positive or negative effect.
Conditioned stimulus	A previously neutral stimulus that elicits the conditioned response because of being repeatedly paired with a stimulus that naturally elicited that response, is called a conditioned stimulus.
Discriminative stimulus	In operant conditioning, a stimulus that indicates that reinforcement is available upon the apporpriate response, is called the discriminative stimulus.
Fixed interval	In a fixed interval schedule of reinforcement, reinforcement occurs after the passage of a specified length of time from the beginning of training or from the last reinforcement, provided that at least one response occurred in that time period.
Deprivation	Deprivation, is the loss or withholding of normal stimulation, nutrition, comfort, love, and so forth; a condition of lacking. The level of stimulation is less than what is required.
Respondent Conditioning	Respondent conditioning refers to behavior that is elicited involuntarily as a reaction to a stimulus. Respondent behavior is identical to classical conditioning UC to UR relationships.
Pavlovian conditioning	Pavlovian conditioning, synonymous with classical conditioning is a type of learning found in animals, caused by the association (or pairing) of two stimuli or what Ivan Pavlov described as the learning of conditional behavior, therefore called conditioning.

Chapter 9. B. F. Skinner

Chapter 10. John Dollard and Neal Miller

Psychoanalysis	Psychoanalysis refers to the school of psychology that emphasizes the importance of unconscious motives and conflicts as determinants of human behavior. It was Freud's method of exploring human personality.
Insight	Insight refers to a sudden awareness of the relationships among various elements that had previously appeared to be independent of one another.
Learning	Learning is a relatively permanent change in behavior that results from experience. Thus, to attribute a behavioral change to learning, the change must be relatively permanent and must result from experience.
Sears	Sears focused on the application of the social learning theory (SLT) to socialization processes, and how children internalize the values, attitudes, and behaviors predominant in their culture. He articulated the place of parents in fostering internalization. In addition, he was among the first social learning theorists to officially acknowledge the reciprocal interaction on an individual's behavior and their environment
Miller and Dollard	Miller and Dollard extended Hull's theory into human social learning conditions. The Social Learning Theory was officially launched in 1941 with their publication of Social Learning and Imitation. It incorporated the principles of Hullian learning: reinforcement, punishment, extinction, and imitation of models.
Social learning	Social learning is learning that occurs as a function of observing, retaining and replicating behavior observed in others. Although social learning can occur at any stage in life, it is thought to be particularly important during childhood, particularly as authority becomes important.
Psychotherapy	Psychotherapy is a set of techniques based on psychological principles intended to improve mental health, emotional or behavioral issues.
Personality	Personality refers to the pattern of enduring characteristics that differentiates a person, the patterns of behaviors that make each individual unique.
Neal Miller	Neal Miller introduced the concepts of the approach gradient and avoidance gradient. Whether organisms drive toward or away from a positive stimulus or a negative stimulus is a function of the distance that it is from that stimulus.
Guthrie	The theory of learning proposed by Guthrie was based on one principle, Contiguity : A combination of stimuli which has accompanied a movement will on its recurrence tend to be followed by that movement. Prediction of behavior will always be probabilistic.
Hull	Hull is best known for the Drive Reduction Theory which postulated that behavior occurs in response to primary drives such as hunger, thirst, sexual interest, etc. When the goal of the drive is attained the drive is reduced. This reduction of drive serves as a reinforcer for learning.
James Rowland Angell	James Rowland Angell is a functional psycholgist interested not only in the operations of mental process considered merely of and by and for itself, but also and more vigorously in mental activity as part of a larger stream of biological forces which are constantly at work.
Physiological psychology	Physiological psychology refers to the study of the physiological mechanisms, in the brain and elsewhere, that mediate behavior and psychological experiences.
Biofeedback	Biofeedback is the process of measuring and quantifying an aspect of a subject's physiology, analyzing the data, and then feeding back the information to the subject in a form that allows the subject to enact physiological change.
Operant Conditioning	A simple form of learning in which an organism learns to engage in behavior because it is reinforced is referred to as operant conditioning. The consequences of a behavior produce changes in the probability of the behavior's occurence.

Chapter 10. John Dollard and Neal Miller

Smooth muscle	Smooth muscle is a type of non-striated muscle, found within the "walls" of hollow organs; such as blood vessels, the bladder, the uterus, and the gastrointestinal tract. Smooth muscle is used to move matter within the body, via contraction; it generally operates "involuntarily", without nerve stimulation.
Gland	A gland is an organ in an animal's body that synthesizes a substance for release such as hormones, often into the bloodstream or into cavities inside the body or its outer surface.
Migraine	Migraine is a form of headache, usually very intense and disabling. It is a neurologic disease.
Brain	The brain controls and coordinates most movement, behavior and homeostatic body functions such as heartbeat, blood pressure, fluid balance and body temperature. Functions of the brain are responsible for cognition, emotion, memory, motor learning and other sorts of learning. The brain is primarily made up of two types of cells: glia and neurons.
Scientific research	Research that is objective, systematic, and testable is called scientific research.
Neuroscience	A field that combines the work of psychologists, biologists, biochemists, medical researchers, and others in the study of the structure and function of the nervous system is neuroscience.
Pavlov	Pavlov first described the phenomenon now known as classical conditioning in experiments with dogs.
Thorndike	Thorndike worked in animal behavior and the learning process leading to the theory of connectionism. Among his most famous contributions were his research on cats escaping from puzzle boxes, and his formulation of the Law of Effect.
Scientific method	Psychologists gather data in order to describe, understand, predict, and control behavior. Scientific method refers to an approach that can be used to discover accurate information. It includes these steps: understand the problem, collect data, draw conclusions, and revise research conclusions.
Social class	Social class describes the relationships between people in hierarchical societies or cultures. Those with more power usually subordinate those with less power.
Innate	Innate behavior is not learned or influenced by the environment, rather, it is present or predisposed at birth.
Overt behavior	An action or response that is directly observable and measurable is an overt behavior.
Displacement	An unconscious defense mechanism in which the individual directs aggressive or sexual feelings away from the primary object to someone or something safe is referred to as displacement. Displacement in linguistics is simply the ability to talk about things not present.
Repression	A defense mechanism, repression involves moving thoughts unacceptable to the ego into the unconscious, where they cannot be easily accessed.
Reinforcer	In operant conditioning, a reinforcer is any stimulus that increases the probability that a preceding behavior will occur again. In Classical Conditioning, the unconditioned stimulus (US) is the reinforcer.
Skinner	Skinner conducted research on shaping behavior through positive and negative reinforcement, and demonstrated operant conditioning, a technique which he developed in contrast with classical conditioning.
Reinforcement	In operant conditioning, reinforcement is any change in an environment that (a) occurs after the behavior, (b) seems to make that behavior re-occur more often in the future and (c) that

Chapter 10. John Dollard and Neal Miller

Chapter 10. John Dollard and Neal Miller

	reoccurence of behavior must be the result of the change.
Drive reduction	Drive reduction theories are based on the need-state. Drive activates behavior. Reinforcement occurs whenever drive is reduced, leading to learning of whatever response solves the need. Thus the reduction in need serves as reinforcement and produces reinforcement of the response that leads to it.
Stimulus	A change in an environmental condition that elicits a response is a stimulus.
Habit	A habit is a response that has become completely separated from its eliciting stimulus. Early learning theorists used the term to describe S-R associations, however not all S-R associations become a habit, rather many are extinguished after reinforcement is withdrawn.
Stimulus generalization	When animals are trained to respond to a single stimulus and test stimuli are introduced that differ from the training stimulus, generally along a single dimension, the systematic decrement in responding typically found has been called the gradient of stimulus generalization.
Secondary Reinforcer	A conditioned reinforcer, sometimes called a secondary reinforcer, is a stimulus or situation that has acquired reinforcing power after being paired in the environment with an unconditioned reinforcer or an earlier conditioned reinforcer.
Pleasure principle	The pleasure principle is the tendency to seek pleasure and avoid pain. In Freud's theory, this principle rules the Id, but is at least partly repressed by the reality principle.
Unconscious mind	The unconscious mind refers to information processing and brain functioning of which a person is unaware. In Freudian theory, it is the repository of unacceptable thoughts and feelings.
Early childhood	Early childhood refers to the developmental period extending from the end of infancy to about 5 or 6 years of age; sometimes called the preschool years.
Variable	A variable refers to a measurable factor, characteristic, or attribute of an individual or a system.
Generalization	In conditioning, the tendency for a conditioned response to be evoked by stimuli that are similar to the stimulus to which the response was conditioned is a generalization. The greater the similarity among the stimuli, the greater the probability of generalization.
Pathology	Pathology is the study of the processes underlying disease and other forms of illness, harmful abnormality, or dysfunction.
Validity	The extent to which a test measures what it is intended to measure is called validity.
Anxiety	Anxiety is a complex combination of the feeling of fear, apprehension and worry often accompanied by physical sensations such as palpitations, chest pain and/or shortness of breath.
Primary drive	A primary drive is a state of tension or arousal arising from a biological or innate need; it is one not based on learning. A primary drive activates behavior.
Acquired drives	Drives acquired through experience, or learned are acquired drives.
Motivation	In psychology, motivation is the driving force (desire) behind all actions of an organism.
Reasoning	Reasoning is the act of using reason to derive a conclusion from certain premises. There are two main methods to reach a conclusion, deductive reasoning and inductive reasoning.
Primary Reinforcer	Any stimulus whose reinforcing effect is immediate and not a function of previous experience is a primary reinforcer (eg, food, water, warmth).
Neutral stimulus	A stimulus prior to conditioning that does not naturally result in the response of interest is called a neutral stimulus.

Chapter 10. John Dollard and Neal Miller

Chapter 10. John Dollard and Neal Miller

Genetics	Genetics is the science of genes, heredity, and the variation of organisms.
Maladaptive	In psychology, a behavior or trait is adaptive when it helps an individual adjust and function well within their social environment. A maladaptive behavior or trait is counterproductive to the individual.
Acquisition	Acquisition is the process of adapting to the environment, learning or becoming conditioned. In classical conditoning terms, it is the initial learning of the stimulus response link, which involves a neutral stimulus being associated with a unconditioned stimulus and becoming a conditioned stimulus.
Phobia	A persistent, irrational fear of an object, situation, or activity that the person feels compelled to avoid is referred to as a phobia.
Punishment	Punishment is the addtion of a stimulus that reduces the frequency of a response, or the removal of a stimulus that results in a reduction of the response.
Extinction	In operant extinction, if no reinforcement is delivered after the response, gradually the behavior will no longer occur in the presence of the stimulus. The process is more rapid following continuous reinforcement rather than after partial reinforcement. In Classical Conditioning, repeated presentations of the CS without being followed by the US results in the extinction of the CS.
Fear response	In the Mowrer-Miller theory, a response to a threatening or noxious situation that is covert but that is assumed to function as a stimulus to produce measurable physiological changes in the body and observable overt behavior is referred to as the fear response.
Discrimination	In Learning theory, discrimination refers the ability to distinguish between a conditioned stimulus and other stimuli. It can be brought about by extensive training or differential reinforcement. In social terms, it is the denial of privileges to a person or a group on the basis of prejudice.
Rape	Rape is a crime where the victim is forced into sexual activity, in particular sexual penetration, against his or her will.
Lewin	Lewin ranks as one of the pioneers of social psychology, as one of the founders of group dynamics and as one of the most eminent representatives of Gestalt psychology.
Superego	Frued's third psychic structure, which functions as a moral guardian and sets forth high standards for behavior is the superego.
Ego	In Freud's view the Ego serves to balance our primitive needs and our moral beliefs and taboos. Relying on experience, a healthy Ego provides the ability to adapt to reality and interact with the outside world.
Approach-approach conflict	A type of conflict in which the goals that produce opposing motives are positive and within reach is referred to as an approach-approach conflict.
Approach-avoidance conflict	Approach-avoidance conflict refers to the tension experienced by people when they are simultaneously attracted to and repulsed by the same goal.
Avoidance-avoidance conflict	A type of conflict in which the goals are negative, but avoidance of one requires approaching the other is an avoidance-avoidance conflict.
Deduction	Deduction refers to reasoning from the general to the particular, as in the case of creating an expected hypothesis for a particular experiment from a general theoretical statement.
Double approach-	Double approach-avoidance conflict refers to being simultaneously attracted to and repelled

Chapter 10. John Dollard and Neal Miller

Chapter 10. John Dollard and Neal Miller

avoidance conflict	by each of two alternatives.
Hypothesis	A specific statement about behavior or mental processes that is testable through research is a hypothesis.
Goal-directed behavior	Goal-directed behavior is means-end problem solving behavior. In the infant, such behavior is first observed in the latter part of the first year.
Behavior modification	Behavior Modification is a technique of altering an individual's reactions to stimuli through positive reinforcement and the extinction of maladaptive behavior.
Verbal Behavior	Verbal Behavior is a book written by B.F. Skinner in which the author presents his ideas on language. For Skinner, speech, along with other forms of communication, was simply a behavior. Skinner argued that each act of speech is an inevitable consequence of the speaker's current environment and his behavioral and sensory history.
Mental processes	The thoughts, feelings, and motives that each of us experiences privately but that cannot be observed directly are called mental processes.
Perception	Perception is the process of acquiring, interpreting, selecting, and organizing sensory information.
Trial and error	Trial and error is an approach to problem solving in which one solution after another is tried in no particular order until an answer is found.
Trait	An enduring personality characteristic that tends to lead to certain behaviors is called a trait. The term trait also means a genetically inherited feature of an organism.
Questionnaire	A self-report method of data collection or clinical assessment method in which the individual being studied checks off items on a printed list, answers multiple-choice questions, or writes out answers to essay questions aimed at producing a selfdescription is called questionnaire.
Consciousness	The awareness of the sensations, thoughts, and feelings being experienced at a given moment is called consciousness.
Neurosis	Neurosis, any mental disorder that, although may cause distress, does not interfere with rational thought or the persons' ability to function.
Society	The social sciences use the term society to mean a group of people that form a semi-closed (or semi-open) social system, in which most interactions are with other individuals belonging to the group.
Compulsion	An apparently irresistible urge to repeat an act or engage in ritualistic behavior such as hand washing is referred to as a compulsion.
Tics	Tics are a repeated, impulsive action, almost reflexive in nature, which the person feels powerless to control or avoid.
Guilt	Guilt describes many concepts related to a negative emotion or condition caused by actions which are believed to be, morally wrong. According to Freud, the avoidance of guilt is the basis for moral behavior.
Transference	Transference is a phenomenon in psychology characterized by unconscious redirection of feelings from one person to another.
Emotion	An emotion is a mental states that arise spontaneously, rather than through conscious effort. They are often accompanied by physiological changes.
Successive approximations	In operant conditioning, a series of behaviors that gradually become more similar to a target behavior are called successive approximations.

Chapter 10. John Dollard and Neal Miller

Catharsis	Catharsis has been adopted by modern psychotherapy as the act of giving expression to deep emotions often associated with events in the individuals past which have never before been adequately expressed.
Oral stage	The oral stage in psychology is the term used by Sigmund Freud to describe the development during the first eighteen months of life, in which an infant's pleasure centers are in the mouth. This is the first of Freud's psychosexual stages.
Attitude	An enduring mental representation of a person, place, or thing that evokes an emotional response and related behavior is called attitude.
Anal stage	The anal stage in psychology is the term used by Sigmund Freud to describe the development during the second year of life, in which a child's pleasure and conflict centers are in the anal area.
Phallic stage	The phallic stage is the 3rd of Freud's psychosexual stages, when awareness of and manipulation of the genitals is supposed to be a primary source of pleasure. In this stage the child deals with the Oedipus complex, if male, or the Electra Complex, if female.
Empirical	Empirical means the use of working hypotheses which are capable of being disproved using observation or experiment.
Theories	Theories are logically self-consistent models or frameworks describing the behavior of a certain natural or social phenomenon. They are broad explanations and predictions concerning phenomena of interest.
Bandura	Bandura is best known for his work on social learning theory or Social Cognitivism. His famous Bobo doll experiment illustrated that people learn from observing others.
Psychoanalyst	A psychoanalyst is a specially trained therapist who attempts to treat the individual by uncovering and revealing to the individual otherwise subconscious factors that are contributing to some undesirable behavor.
Overgenerali-ation	Overgeneralization is concluding that all instances of some kind of event will turn out a certain way because one or more in the past did. For instance, a class goes badly one day and I conclude, "I'll never be a good teacher."
Psychoanalytic	Freud's theory that unconscious forces act as determinants of personality is called psychoanalytic theory. The theory is a developmental theory characterized by critical stages of development.
Behavior therapy	Behavior therapy refers to the systematic application of the principles of learning to direct modification of a client's problem behaviors.
Human nature	Human nature is the fundamental nature and substance of humans, as well as the range of human behavior that is believed to be invariant over long periods of time and across very different cultural contexts.
Displaced aggression	Redirecting aggression to a target other than the actual source of one's frustration is a defense mechanism called displaced aggression.

Chapter 10. John Dollard and Neal Miller

Chapter 11. Albert Bandura and Walter Mischel

Social cognitive theory	Social cognitive theory defines human behavior as a triadic, dynamic, and reciprocal interaction of personal factors, behavior, and the environment. Response consequences of a behavior are used to form expectations of behavioral outcomes. It is the ability to form these expectations that give humans the capability to predict the outcomes of their behavior, before the behavior is performed.
Bandura	Bandura is best known for his work on social learning theory or Social Cognitivism. His famous Bobo doll experiment illustrated that people learn from observing others.
Mischel	Mischel is known for his cognitive social learning model of personality that focuses on the specific cognitive variables that mediate the manner in which new experiences affect the individual.
Motivation	In psychology, motivation is the driving force (desire) behind all actions of an organism.
Affect	A subjective feeling or emotional tone often accompanied by bodily expressions noticeable to others is called affect.
Psychopathology	Psychopathology refers to the field concerned with the nature and development of mental disorders.
Observational learning	The acquisition of knowledge and skills through the observation of others rather than by means of direct experience is observational learning. Four major processes are thought to influence the observational learning: attentional, retentional, behavioral production, and motivational.
Personality	Personality refers to the pattern of enduring characteristics that differentiates a person, the patterns of behaviors that make each individual unique.
Principles of Behavior	Hull published Principles of Behavior, in 1943. His theory is characterized by very strict operationalization of variables and mathematical presentation. The essence of the theory can be summarized by saying that the response is a function of the strength of the habit times the strength of the drive. It is for this reason that Hull's theory is often referred to as drive theory.
Social learning	Social learning is learning that occurs as a function of observing, retaining and replicating behavior observed in others. Although social learning can occur at any stage in life, it is thought to be particularly important during childhood, particularly as authority becomes important.
Self-efficacy	Self-efficacy is the belief that one has the capabilities to execute the courses of actions required to manage prospective situations.
Learning	Learning is a relatively permanent change in behavior that results from experience. Thus, to attribute a behavioral change to learning, the change must be relatively permanent and must result from experience.
American Psychological Association	The American Psychological Association is a professional organization representing psychology in the US. The mission statement is to "advance psychology as a science and profession and as a means of promoting health, education, and human welfare".
James McKeen Cattell	James McKeen Cattell was the first professor of psychology in the United States. His major contribution to psychology was the realization of the importance, and subsequent implementation, of quantitative methodologies and techniques. He coined the term "mental test" 1890.
Clinical psychology	Clinical psychology is involved in the diagnosis, assessment, and treatment of patients with mental or behavioral disorders, and conducts research in these various areas.
Society	The social sciences use the term society to mean a group of people that form a semi-closed

Chapter 11. Albert Bandura and Walter Mischel

Chapter 11. Albert Bandura and Walter Mischel

	(or semi-open) social system, in which most interactions are with other individuals belonging to the group.
Psychoanalysis	Psychoanalysis refers to the school of psychology that emphasizes the importance of unconscious motives and conflicts as determinants of human behavior. It was Freud's method of exploring human personality.
Juvenile delinquent	An adolescent who breaks the law or engages in behavior that is considered illegal is referred to as a juvenile delinquent.
Psychoanalytic	Freud's theory that unconscious forces act as determinants of personality is called psychoanalytic theory. The theory is a developmental theory characterized by critical stages of development.
George Kelly	George Kelly developed his major contribution to the psychology of personality, The Psychology of Personal Constructs in 1955 and achieved immediate international recognition. He worked in clinical school psychology, developing a program of traveling clinics which also served as a training ground for his students.
Rotter	Rotter focused on the application of social learning theory (SLT) to clinical psychology. She introduced the ideas of learning from generalized expectancies of reinforcement and internal/ external locus of control (self-initiated change versus change influenced by others). According to Rotter, health outcomes could be improved by the development of a sense of personal control over one's life.
Construct	A generalized concept, such as anxiety or gravity, is a construct.
Trait	An enduring personality characteristic that tends to lead to certain behaviors is called a trait. The term trait also means a genetically inherited feature of an organism.
Cognitive psychology	Cognitive psychology is the psychological science which studies the mental processes that are hypothesised to underlie behavior. This covers a broad range of research domains, examining questions about the workings of memory, attention, perception, knowledge representation, reasoning, creativity and problem solving.
Personality test	A personality test aims to describe aspects of a person's character that remain stable across situations.
Questionnaire	A self-report method of data collection or clinical assessment method in which the individual being studied checks off items on a printed list, answers multiple-choice questions, or writes out answers to essay questions aimed at producing a selfdescription is called questionnaire.
Fixation	Fixation in abnormal psychology is the state where an individual becomes obsessed with an attachment to another human, animal or inanimate object. Fixation in vision refers to maintaining the gaze in a constant direction. .
Trait theory	According to trait theory, personality can be broken down into a limited number of traits, which are present in each individual to a greater or lesser degree. This approach is highly compatible with the quantitative psychometric approach to personality testing.
Reinforcement	In operant conditioning, reinforcement is any change in an environment that (a) occurs after the behavior, (b) seems to make that behavior re-occur more often in the future and (c) that reoccurence of behavior must be the result of the change.
Individual differences	Individual differences psychology studies the ways in which individual people differ in their behavior. This is distinguished from other aspects of psychology in that although psychology is ostensibly a study of individuals, modern psychologists invariably study groups.
Correlation	A statistical technique for determining the degree of association between two or more

Go to Cram101.com for the Practice Tests for this Chapter.

Chapter 11. Albert Bandura and Walter Mischel

Chapter 11. Albert Bandura and Walter Mischel

	variables is referred to as correlation.
Perception	Perception is the process of acquiring, interpreting, selecting, and organizing sensory information.
Variable	A variable refers to a measurable factor, characteristic, or attribute of an individual or a system.
Maladaptive	In psychology, a behavior or trait is adaptive when it helps an individual adjust and function well within their social environment. A maladaptive behavior or trait is counterproductive to the individual.
Theories	Theories are logically self-consistent models or frameworks describing the behavior of a certain natural or social phenomenon. They are broad explanations and predictions concerning phenomena of interest.
Habit	A habit is a response that has become completely separated from its eliciting stimulus. Early learning theorists used the term to describe S-R associations, however not all S-R associations become a habit, rather many are extinguished after reinforcement is withdrawn.
Skinner	Skinner conducted research on shaping behavior through positive and negative reinforcement, and demonstrated operant conditioning, a technique which he developed in contrast with classical conditioning.
Reciprocal Determinism	Bandura's term for the social-cognitive view that people influence their environment just as their environment influences them is reciprocal determinism.
Physical attractiveness	Physical attractiveness is the perception of an individual as physically beautiful by other people.
Physiognomy	Physiognomy is a pseudoscience, based upon the belief that the study and judgement of a person's outer appearance, primarily the face, reflects their character or personality.
Individualistic	Cultures have been classified as individualistic, which means having a set of values that give priority to personal goals rather than group goals.
Stimulus	A change in an environmental condition that elicits a response is a stimulus.
Encoding	Encoding refers to interpreting; transforming; modifying information so that it can be placed in memory. It is the first stage of information processing.
Assertiveness	Assertiveness basically means the ability to express your thoughts and feelings in a way that clearly states your needs and keeps the lines of communication open with the other.
Hypothesis	A specific statement about behavior or mental processes that is testable through research is a hypothesis.
Punishment	Punishment is the addtion of a stimulus that reduces the frequency of a response, or the removal of a stimulus that results in a reduction of the response.
Self-Regulatory	Bandura proposes that self-regulatory systems mediate external influences and provide a basis for purposeful action, allowing people to have personal control over their own thoughts, feelings, motivations, and actions.
Bobo doll	The Bobo doll experiment was conducted by Bandura to study aggressive patterns of behavior. One of the experiment's conclusions was that people can learn through vicarious reinforcement.
Control group	A group that does not receive the treatment effect in an experiment is referred to as the control group or sometimes as the comparison group.
Incentive	An incentive is what is expected once a behavior is performed. An incentive acts as a

Chapter 11. Albert Bandura and Walter Mischel

Chapter 11. Albert Bandura and Walter Mischel

	reinforcer.
Trial and error	Trial and error is an approach to problem solving in which one solution after another is tried in no particular order until an answer is found.
Corporal punishment	Corporal punishment is the use of physical force with the intention of causing pain, but not injury.
Social influence	Social influence is when the actions or thoughts of individual(s) are changed by other individual(s). Peer pressure is an example of social influence.
Attentional processes	In Bandura's theory of vicarious learning, any activity by an observer that aids in the observation of relevant aspects of a model's behavior and its consequences is referred to as attentional processes.
Attention	Attention is the cognitive process of selectively concentrating on one thing while ignoring other things. Psychologists have labeled three types of attention: sustained attention, selective attention, and divided attention.
Retentional processes	Effectiveness of observational learning depends in part on retentional processes. To retain what has been attended to, individuals must somehow encode the information into long-term memory. According to Bandura, humans store the behaviors they observe in the form of mental images or verbal descriptions.
Motor reproduction	Motor reproduction involves converting symbolic representation into overt behavior and is essential for effective observational learning.
Behavioral Production	Behavioral production or motor reproduction is another process in observational learning. The observer must be able to reproduce the model's behavior. The observer must learn and posses the physical capabilities of the modeled behavior.
Feedback	Feedback refers to information returned to a person about the effects a response has had.
Motivational processes	In observational learning, the motivational processes are the degree to which a behavior is seen to result in a valued outcome (expectancies) will influence the likelihood that one will adopt a modeled behavior.
Vicarious reinforcement	A behavior response that increases as a result of observing other people's behaviors being reinforced is referred to as vicarious reinforcement.
Intrinsic Reinforcement	In intrinsic reinforcement the reinforcer occurs within the individual. Behavior maintained by intrinsic reinforcement tends to be more resistant to extinction.
Depression	In everyday language depression refers to any downturn in mood, which may be relatively transitory and perhaps due to something trivial. This is differentiated from Clinical depression which is marked by symptoms that last two weeks or more and are so severe that they interfere with daily living.
Chronic	Chronic refers to a relatively long duration, usually more than a few months.
Emotion	An emotion is a mental states that arise spontaneously, rather than through conscious effort. They are often accompanied by physiological changes.
Psychotherapy	Psychotherapy is a set of techniques based on psychological principles intended to improve mental health, emotional or behavioral issues.
Euphemistic Labeling	Euphemistic Labeling is the calling of an otherwise reprehensible act something other than what it really is. It enables the person to act without self-contempt.
Prejudice	Prejudice in general, implies coming to a judgment on the subject before learning where the preponderance of the evidence actually lies, or formation of a judgement without direct experience.

Chapter 11. Albert Bandura and Walter Mischel

Chapter 11. Albert Bandura and Walter Mischel

Advantageous Comparison	Advantageous comparison is a practice that is widely employed where one's aggressive actions are compared with more heinous outcomes to minimize the negativity of their own actions.
Displacement of responsibility	The "I was only following orders" defense, is MIlgram's displacement of responsibility effect. People seem able to suspend moral judgement if a legitimate authority accepts responsibility for their actions.
Diffusion of responsibility	Diffusion of responsibility is a social phenomenon which tends to occur in groups of people above a certain critical size when responsibility is not explicitly assigned.
Rape	Rape is a crime where the victim is forced into sexual activity, in particular sexual penetration, against his or her will.
Aptitude test	A test designed to predict a person's ability in a particular area or line of work is called an aptitude test.
Quantitative	A quantitative property is one that exists in a range of magnitudes, and can therefore be measured. Measurements of any particular quantitative property are expressed as as a specific quantity, referred to as a unit, multiplied by a number.
Participant modeling	A behavior therapy in which an appropriate response is modeled in graduated steps and the client attempts each step, encouraged and supported by the therapist is participant modeling.
Self-efficacy expectations	Beliefs to the effect that one can handle a task, that one can bring about desired changes through one's own efforts are called self-efficacy expectations.
Phobia	A persistent, irrational fear of an object, situation, or activity that the person feels compelled to avoid is referred to as a phobia.
Anxiety	Anxiety is a complex combination of the feeling of fear, apprehension and worry often accompanied by physical sensations such as palpitations, chest pain and/or shortness of breath.
Desensitization	Desensitization refers to the type of sensory or behavioral adaptation in which we become less sensitive to constant stimuli.
Free will	The idea that human beings are capable of freely making choices or decisions is free will.
William James	Functionalism as a psychology developed out of Pragmatism as a philosophy: To find the meaning of an idea, you have to look at its consequences. This led William James and his students towards an emphasis on cause and effect, prediction and control, and observation of environment and behavior, over the careful introspection of the Structuralists.
Determinism	Determinism is the philosophical proposition that every event, including human cognition and action, is causally determined by an unbroken chain of prior occurrences.
Motives	Needs or desires that energize and direct behavior toward a goal are motives.
Mind-body relationship	Mind-body relationship is the philosophical issue regarding whether the mind and body operate indistinguishably as a single system or whether they act as two separate systems.
Dualism	Dualism is a set of beliefs which begins with the claim that the mental and the physical have a fundamentally different nature. It is contrasted with varying kinds of monism, including materialism and phenomenalism. Dualism is one answer to the mind-body problem.
Brain	The brain controls and coordinates most movement, behavior and homeostatic body functions such as heartbeat, blood pressure, fluid balance and body temperature. Functions of the brain are responsible for cognition, emotion, memory, motor learning and other sorts of learning. The brain is primarily made up of two types of cells: glia and neurons.
Reductionism	Reductionism holds that the nature of complex things can always be reduced to (be explained by) simpler or more fundamental things.

Chapter 11. Albert Bandura and Walter Mischel

Chapter 11. Albert Bandura and Walter Mischel

Empirical	Empirical means the use of working hypotheses which are capable of being disproved using observation or experiment.
Correlational method	A research method used to establish the degree of relationship between two characteristics, events, or behaviors is called a correlational method.
Bem	Bem is the originator of the self-perception theory of attitude change. According to the self-perception account, people infer their attitudes about others from their own behavior and its causes.
Population	Population refers to all members of a well-defined group of organisms, events, or things.
Situational determinants	The environmental conditions that precede and follow a particular piece of behavior, a primary focus of behavioral assessment are situational determinants.
Allport	Allport was a trait theorist. Those traits he believed to predominate a person's personality were called central traits. Traits such that one could be indentifed by the trait, were referred to as cardinal traits. Central traits and cardinal traits are influenced by environmental factors.
Unconscious mind	The unconscious mind refers to information processing and brain functioning of which a person is unaware. In Freudian theory, it is the repository of unacceptable thoughts and feelings.
Psychoanalyst	A psychoanalyst is a specially trained therapist who attempts to treat the individual by uncovering and revealing to the individual otherwise subconscious factors that are contributing to some undesirable behavor.
Heuristic	A heuristic is a simple, efficient rule of thumb proposed to explain how people make decisions, come to judgments and solve problems, typically when facing complex problems or incomplete information. These rules work well under most circumstances, but in certain cases lead to systematic cognitive biases.
Goal-directed behavior	Goal-directed behavior is means-end problem solving behavior. In the infant, such behavior is first observed in the latter part of the first year.
Moral development	Development regarding rules and conventions about what people should do in their interactions with other people is called moral development.
Reinforcer	In operant conditioning, a reinforcer is any stimulus that increases the probability that a preceding behavior will occur again. In Classical Conditioning, the unconditioned stimulus (US) is the reinforcer.
Extrinsic Reinforcement	Extrinsic Reinforcement means that the reinforcing stimulus is produced in the external environment.

Chapter 11. Albert Bandura and Walter Mischel

Chapter 12. Edward O. Wilson

Edward O. Wilson	Edward O. Wilson is an entomologist and biologist known for his work on ecology, evolution, and sociobiology. Sociobiology suggests that animal, and by extension human, behavior can be studied using an evolutionary framework.
Sociobiology	Sociobiology is a synthesis of scientific disciplines that attempts to explain behavior in all species by considering the evolutionary advantages of social behaviors.
Altruism	Altruism is being helpful to other people with little or no interest in being rewarded for one's efforts. This is distinct from merely helping others.
Suicide	Suicide behavior is rare in childhood but escalates in adolescence. The suicide rate increases in a linear fashion from adolescence through late adulthood.
Evolution	Commonly used to refer to gradual change, evolution is the change in the frequency of alleles within a population from one generation to the next. This change may be caused by different mechanisms, including natural selection, genetic drift, or changes in population (gene flow).
Evolutionary psychology	Evolutionary psychology proposes that cognition and behavior can be better understood in light of evolutionary history.
Acute	Acute means sudden, sharp, and abrupt. Usually short in duration.
Human nature	Human nature is the fundamental nature and substance of humans, as well as the range of human behavior that is believed to be invariant over long periods of time and across very different cultural contexts.
Evolutionary theory	Evolutionary theory is concerned with heritable variability rather than behavioral variations. Natural selection requirements: (1) natural variability within a species must exist, (2) only some individual differences are heritable, and (3) natural selection only takes place when there is an interaction between the inborn attributes of organisms and the environment in which they live.
American Psychological Association	The American Psychological Association is a professional organization representing psychology in the US. The mission statement is to "advance psychology as a science and profession and as a means of promoting health, education , and human welfare".
Darwin	Darwin achieved lasting fame as originator of the theory of evolution through natural selection. His book Expression of Emotions in Man and Animals is generally considered the first text on comparative psychology.
Species	Species refers to a reproductively isolated breeding population.
Individual differences	Individual differences psychology studies the ways in which individual people differ in their behavior. This is distinguished from other aspects of psychology in that although psychology is ostensibly a study of individuals, modern psychologists invariably study groups.
Adaptation	Adaptation is a lowering of sensitivity to a stimulus following prolonged exposure to that stimulus. Behavioral adaptations are special ways a particular organism behaves to survive in its natural habitat.
Trait	An enduring personality characteristic that tends to lead to certain behaviors is called a trait. The term trait also means a genetically inherited feature of an organism.
Reproductive fitness	Reproductive Fitness refers to the reproductive success of an individual organism relative to the average reproductive success of the population.
Natural selection	Natural selection is a process by which biological populations are altered over time, as a result of the propagation of heritable traits that affect the capacity of individual organisms to survive and reproduce.
Inclusive	Inclusive fitness is the sum of an individual's own reproductive success plus the effects the

Chapter 12. Edward O. Wilson

Chapter 12. Edward O. Wilson

fitness	organism has on the reproductive success of related others.
Gene	A gene is an ultramicroscopic area of the chromosome. It is the smallest physical unit of the DNA molecule that carries a piece of hereditary information.
Brain	The brain controls and coordinates most movement, behavior and homeostatic body functions such as heartbeat, blood pressure, fluid balance and body temperature. Functions of the brain are responsible for cognition, emotion, memory, motor learning and other sorts of learning. The brain is primarily made up of two types of cells: glia and neurons.
Personality	Personality refers to the pattern of enduring characteristics that differentiates a person, the patterns of behaviors that make each individual unique.
Theories	Theories are logically self-consistent models or frameworks describing the behavior of a certain natural or social phenomenon. They are broad explanations and predictions concerning phenomena of interest.
Empirical	Empirical means the use of working hypotheses which are capable of being disproved using observation or experiment.
Locke	In 1690, Locke wrote his Essay Concerning Human Understanding. The essay arugued for empiricism, that ideas come only from experience. In other words, there are no innate ideas. The tabula rasa or blank slate was his metaphor.
Tabula rasa	In Locke's philosophy, Tabula rasa is the notion that individual human beings are born "blank" (with no built-in mental content), and that their identity is defined entirely by events after birth.
Innate	Innate behavior is not learned or influenced by the environment, rather, it is present or predisposed at birth.
Reinforcement contingencies	The circumstances or rules that determine whether responses lead to the presentation of reinforcers are referred to as reinforcement contingencies. Skinner defined culture as a set of reinforcement contingencies.
Reinforcement	In operant conditioning, reinforcement is any change in an environment that (a) occurs after the behavior, (b) seems to make that behavior re-occur more often in the future and (c) that reoccurence of behavior must be the result of the change.
Habit	A habit is a response that has become completely separated from its eliciting stimulus. Early learning theorists used the term to describe S-R associations, however not all S-R associations become a habit, rather many are extinguished after reinforcement is withdrawn.
Verbal Behavior	Verbal Behavior is a book written by B.F. Skinner in which the author presents his ideas on language. For Skinner, speech, along with other forms of communication, was simply a behavior. Skinner argued that each act of speech is an inevitable consequence of the speaker's current environment and his behavioral and sensory history.
Biogrammar	Evolutionary psychology uses the term biogrammar to describe Bolles' notion that there is an innate structure that guides learning according to predispositions, and that learning is prepared according to evolutionary history.
Adaptive behavior	An adaptive behavior increases the probability of the individual or organism to survive or exist within its environment.
Causation	Causation concerns the time order relationship between two or more objects such that if a specific antecendent condition occurs the same consequent must always follow.
Motivational state	A motivational state is an internal, reversible condition in an individual that orients the individual toward one or another type of goal. This condition is not observed directly but is inferred from the individual's behavior.

Go to **Cram101.com** for the Practice Tests for this Chapter.

Chapter 12. Edward O. Wilson

Chapter 12. Edward O. Wilson

Learning	Learning is a relatively permanent change in behavior that results from experience. Thus, to attribute a behavioral change to learning, the change must be relatively permanent and must result from experience.
Ultimate explanations	Ultimate explanations are functional explanations of behavior that state the role that the behavior plays or once played in survival and reproduction. They explain why the behavior was favored by natural selection.
Attachment	Attachment is the tendency to seek closeness to another person and feel secure when that person is present.
Biological Determinism	Biological Determinism refers to the type of determinism that stresses the biochemical, genetic, physiological, or anatomical causes of behavior
Insanity	A legal status indicating that a person cannot be held responsible for his or her actions because of mental illness is called insanity.
Predisposition	Predisposition refers to an inclination or diathesis to respond in a certain way, either inborn or acquired. In abnormal psychology, it is a factor that lowers the ability to withstand stress and inclines the individual toward pathology.
Mind-body relationship	Mind-body relationship is the philosophical issue regarding whether the mind and body operate indistinguishably as a single system or whether they act as two separate systems.
Consciousness	The awareness of the sensations, thoughts, and feelings being experienced at a given moment is called consciousness.
Society	The social sciences use the term society to mean a group of people that form a semi-closed (or semi-open) social system, in which most interactions are with other individuals belonging to the group.
Mind-body problem	There are three basic views of the mind-body problem: mental and physical events are totally different, and cannot be reduced to each other (dualism); mental events are to be reduced to physical events (materialism); and physical events are to be reduced to mental events (phenomenalism).
Emotion	An emotion is a mental states that arise spontaneously, rather than through conscious effort. They are often accompanied by physiological changes.
Perception	Perception is the process of acquiring, interpreting, selecting, and organizing sensory information.
Sensation	Sensation is the first stage in the chain of biochemical and neurologic events that begins with the impinging of a stimulus upon the receptor cells of a sensory organ, which then leads to perception, the mental state that is reflected in statements like "I see a uniformly blue wall."
Information processing	Information processing is an approach to the goal of understanding human thinking. The essence of the approach is to see cognition as being essentially computational in nature, with mind being the software and the brain being the hardware.
Prepared learning	Prepared learning is a concept that suggests certain associations can be learned more readily than others because this ability has been adaptive for the organism.
Preparedness	The species-specific biological predisposition to learn in certain ways is called preparedness.
Phobia	A persistent, irrational fear of an object, situation, or activity that the person feels compelled to avoid is referred to as a phobia.
Kin selection	Kin selection has been mathematically defined by Hamilton as a mechanism for the evolution of

Chapter 12. Edward O. Wilson

apparently altruistic acts. Under natural selection, a gene that causes itself to increase in frequency should become more common in the population. Since identical copies of genes may be carried in relatives, a gene in one organism that prompts behavior which aids another organism carrying the same gene may become more successful.

Trivers	Trivers is most noted for proposing the theories of reciprocal altruism, parental investment, and parent-offspring conflict. Other areas in which he has made influential contributions include an adaptive view of self-deception and intragenomic conflict.
Reciprocity	Reciprocity, in interpersonal attraction, is the tendency to return feelings and attitudes that are expressed about us.
Discrimination	In Learning theory, discrimination refers the ability to distinguish between a conditioned stimulus and other stimuli. It can be brought about by extensive training or differential reinforcement. In social terms, it is the denial of privileges to a person or a group on the basis of prejudice.
Variable	A variable refers to a measurable factor, characteristic, or attribute of an individual or a system.
Placenta	A membrane that permits the exchange of nutrients and waste products between the mother and her developing child but does not allow the maternal and fetal bloodstreams to mix is the placenta.
Embryo	A developed zygote that has a rudimentary heart, brain, and other organs is referred to as an embryo.
Refractory period	Refractory period refers to a phase following firing during which a neuron is less sensitive to messages from other neurons and will not fire. In the sexual response cycle, it is a period of time following orgasm during which an individual is not responsive to sexual stimulation.
Polygyny	Polygyny is a marital practice in which a man has more than one wife simultaneously.
Polyandry	A mating system in which each female seeks to mate with multiple males, while each male mates with only one female is referred to as polyandry.
Chromosome	The DNA which carries genetic information in biological cells is normally packaged in the form of one or more large macromolecules called a chromosome. Humans normally have 46.
Motives	Needs or desires that energize and direct behavior toward a goal are motives.
Ovulation	Ovulation is the process in the menstrual cycle by which a mature ovarian follicle ruptures and discharges an ovum (also known as an oocyte, female gamete, or casually, an egg) that participates in reproduction.
Estrus	The estrus cycle refers to the recurring physiologic changes that are induced by reproductive hormones in most mammalian placental females (humans and great apes are the only mammals who undergo a menstrual cycle instead).
Socioeconomic Status	A family's socioeconomic status is based on family income, parental education level, parental occupation, and social status in the community. Those with high status often have more success in preparing their children for school because they have access to a wide range of resources.
Wisdom	Wisdom is the ability to make correct judgments and decisions. It is an intangible quality gained through experience. Whether or not something is wise is determined in a pragmatic sense by its popularity, how long it has been around, and its ability to predict against future events.
Ethnocentrism	Ethnocentrism is the tendency to look at the world primarily from the perspective of one's

Chapter 12. Edward O. Wilson

	own culture.
Social isolation	Social isolation refers to a type of loneliness that occurs when a person lacks a sense of integrated involvement. Being deprived of participation in a group or community involving companionship, shared interests, organized activities, and meaningful roles causes a person to feel alone.
Early adulthood	The developmental period beginning in the late teens or early twenties and lasting into the thirties is called early adulthood; characterized by an increasing self-awareness.
Adolescence	The period of life bounded by puberty and the assumption of adult responsibilities is adolescence.
Punishment	Punishment is the addtion of a stimulus that reduces the frequency of a response, or the removal of a stimulus that results in a reduction of the response.
Xenophobia	Xenophobia denotes a phobic attitude toward strangers or of the unknown.
Validity	The extent to which a test measures what it is intended to measure is called validity.
Evolutionary perspective	A perspective that focuses on how humans have evolved and adapted behaviors required for survival against various environmental pressures over the long course is called the evolutionary perspective.
Socialization	Social rules and social relations are created, communicated, and changed in verbal and nonverbal ways creating social complexity useful in identifying outsiders and intelligent breeding partners. The process of learning these skills is called socialization.
Masturbation	Masturbation is the manual excitation of the sexual organs, most often to the point of orgasm. It can refer to excitation either by oneself or by another, but commonly refers to such activities performed alone.
Incest	Incest refers to sexual relations between close relatives, most often between daughter and father or between brother and sister.
Rape	Rape is a crime where the victim is forced into sexual activity, in particular sexual penetration, against his or her will.
Homosexual	Homosexual refers to a sexual orientation characterized by aesthetic attraction, romantic love, and sexual desire exclusively for members of the same sex or gender identity.
Psychoanalysis	Psychoanalysis refers to the school of psychology that emphasizes the importance of unconscious motives and conflicts as determinants of human behavior. It was Freud's method of exploring human personality.
Ego	In Freud's view the Ego serves to balance our primitive needs and our moral beliefs and taboos. Relying on experience, a healthy Ego provides the ability to adapt to reality and interact with the outside world.
Superego	Frued's third psychic structure, which functions as a moral guardian and sets forth high standards for behavior is the superego.
Ego ideal	The component of the superego that involves ideal standards approved by parents is called ego ideal. The ego ideal rewards the child by conveying a sense of pride and personal value when the child acts according to ideal standards.
Guilt	Guilt describes many concepts related to a negative emotion or condition caused by actions which are believed to be, morally wrong. According to Freud, the avoidance of guilt is the basis for moral behavior.
Norms	In testing, standards of test performance that permit the comparison of one person's score on the test to the scores of others who have taken the same test are referred to as norms.

Chapter 12. Edward O. Wilson

Chapter 12. Edward O. Wilson

Unconscious mind	The unconscious mind refers to information processing and brain functioning of which a person is unaware. In Freudian theory, it is the repository of unacceptable thoughts and feelings.
Archetype	The archetype is a concept of psychologist Carl Jung. They are innate prototypes for ideas, which may subsequently become involved in the interpretation of observed phenomena. A group of memories and interpretations closely associated with an archetype is called a complex.
Jung	Jung was in some aspects a response to Sigmund Freud's psychoanalysis. He proposed and developed the concepts of the extroverted and introverted personality, archetypes, and the collective unconscious. His work has been influential in psychiatry and in the study of religion, literature, and related fields.
Stephen Jay Gould	Stephen Jay Gould helped Niles Eldredge develop the theory of punctuated equilibrium in 1972, wherein evolutionary change occurs relatively rapidly in comparatively brief periods of environmental stress, separated by longer periods of evolutionary stability.
Eugenics	The field concerned with improving the hereditary qualities of the human race through social control of mating and reproduction is called eugenics.
Naturalistic observation	Naturalistic observation is a method of observation that involves observing subjects in their natural habitats. Researchers take great care in avoiding making interferences with the behavior they are observing by using unobtrusive methods.
Spandrels	In evolutionary psychology, spandrels are phenotypic characteristics that evolved as a side effect of a true adaptation.
Kamin	Kamin argues that blocking is caused by lack of learning. In the compound stimulus training, there is lack of surprise about the outcome because one of the members of the compound stimulus already predicts the outcome. There is no surprise effect, therefore no learning.
Naturalistic fallacy	Moore coined the term naturalistic fallacy to describe arguments which claim to draw ethical conclusions from the fact that something is "natural" or "unnatural."
Genetics	Genetics is the science of genes, heredity, and the variation of organisms.
Biological predisposition	The genetic readiness of animals and humans to perform certain behaviors is a biological predisposition.
Correlation	A statistical technique for determining the degree of association between two or more variables is referred to as correlation.
Parental investment	Robert Trivers' theory of parental investment predicts that the sex making the largest investment in lactation, nurturing and protecting offspring will be more discriminating in mating and that the sex that invests less in offspring will compete for access to the higher investing sex.
Physiology	The study of the functions and activities of living cells, tissues, and organs and of the physical and chemical phenomena involved is referred to as physiology.
Anatomy	Anatomy is the branch of biology that deals with the structure and organization of living things. It can be divided into animal anatomy (zootomy) and plant anatomy (phytonomy). Major branches of anatomy include comparative anatomy, histology, and human anatomy.
Sexism	Sexism is commonly considered to be discrimination against people based on their sex rather than their individual merits, but can also refer to any and all differentiations based on
Heuristic	A heuristic is a simple, efficient rule of thumb proposed to explain how people make decisions, come to judgments and solve problems, typically when facing complex problems or incomplete information. These rules work well under most circumstances, but in certain cases lead to systematic cognitive biases.

Chapter 12. Edward O. Wilson

Chapter 12. Edward O. Wilson

Comparative psychology	Comparative psychology is the study of the behavior of animals in order to infer similar functionaility in humans.
Population	Population refers to all members of a well-defined group of organisms, events, or things.
Ethology	Where comparative psychology sees the study of animal behavior in the context of what is known about human psychology, ethology sees the study of animal behavior in the context of what is known about animal anatomy and physiology.
Ecology	Ecology refers to the branch of biology that deals with the relationships between living organisms and their environment.
Behaviorism	The school of psychology that defines psychology as the study of observable behavior and studies relationships between stimuli and responses is called behaviorism. Behaviorism relied heavily on animal research and stated the same principles governed the behavior of both nonhumans and humans.
Conformity	Conformity is the degree to which members of a group will change their behavior, views and attitudes to fit the views of the group. The group can influence members via unconscious processes or via overt social pressure on individuals.
Illusion	An illusion is a distortion of a sensory perception.
Metaphor	A metaphor is a rhetorical trope where a comparison is made between two seemingly unrelated subjects
Reflection	Reflection is the process of rephrasing or repeating thoughts and feelings expressed, making the person more aware of what they are saying or thinking.
Extinction	In operant extinction, if no reinforcement is delivered after the response, gradually the behavior will no longer occur in the presence of the stimulus. The process is more rapid following continuous reinforcement rather than after partial reinforcement. In Classical Conditioning, repeated presentations of the CS without being followed by the US results in the extinction of the CS.

Go to Cram101.com for the Practice Tests for this Chapter.

Chapter 12. Edward O. Wilson

Chapter 13. George Kelly

Stimulus-response psychology	Stimulus-response psychology regards all behavior as a series of responses to different stimuli. In theory, any stimulus connected with any response can eventually be identified. It regards behavior as predictable and potentially controllable.
Pathology	Pathology is the study of the processes underlying disease and other forms of illness, harmful abnormality, or dysfunction.
Depression	In everyday language depression refers to any downturn in mood, which may be relatively transitory and perhaps due to something trivial. This is differentiated from Clinical depression which is marked by symptoms that last two weeks or more and are so severe that they interfere with daily living.
Clinical psychology	Clinical psychology is involved in the diagnosis, assessment, and treatment of patients with mental or behavioral disorders, and conducts research in these various areas.
Psychotherapy	Psychotherapy is a set of techniques based on psychological principles intended to improve mental health, emotional or behavioral issues.
Insight	Insight refers to a sudden awareness of the relationships among various elements that had previously appeared to be independent of one another.
Personality	Personality refers to the pattern of enduring characteristics that differentiates a person, the patterns of behaviors that make each individual unique.
Theories	Theories are logically self-consistent models or frameworks describing the behavior of a certain natural or social phenomenon. They are broad explanations and predictions concerning phenomena of interest.
Rotter	Rotter focused on the application of social learning theory (SLT) to clinical psychology. She introduced the ideas of learning from generalized expectancies of reinforcement and internal/external locus of control (self-initiated change versus change influenced by others). According to Rotter, health outcomes could be improved by the development of a sense of personal control over one's life.
Ecology	Ecology refers to the branch of biology that deals with the relationships between living organisms and their environment.
American Psychological Association	The American Psychological Association is a professional organization representing psychology in the US. The mission statement is to "advance psychology as a science and profession and as a means of promoting health, education, and human welfare".
Construct	A generalized concept, such as anxiety or gravity, is a construct.
Reinforcement	In operant conditioning, reinforcement is any change in an environment that (a) occurs after the behavior, (b) seems to make that behavior re-occur more often in the future and (c) that reoccurence of behavior must be the result of the change.
Motivation	In psychology, motivation is the driving force (desire) behind all actions of an organism.
Emotion	An emotion is a mental states that arise spontaneously, rather than through conscious effort. They are often accompanied by physiological changes.
Ego	In Freud's view the Ego serves to balance our primitive needs and our moral beliefs and taboos. Relying on experience, a healthy Ego provides the ability to adapt to reality and interact with the outside world.
Creativity	Creativity is the ability to think about something in novel and unusual ways and come up with unique solutions to problems. It involves divergent thinking, having many solutions or views to a problem.
Guilt	Guilt describes many concepts related to a negative emotion or condition caused by actions

Chapter 13. George Kelly

Chapter 13. George Kelly

	which are believed to be, morally wrong. According to Freud, the avoidance of guilt is the basis for moral behavior.
Clinical psychologist	A psychologist, usually with a Ph.D, whose training is in the diagnosis, treatment, or research of psychological and behavioral disorders is a clinical psychologist.
Psychoanalytic	Freud's theory that unconscious forces act as determinants of personality is called psychoanalytic theory. The theory is a developmental theory characterized by critical stages of development.
Trait theory	According to trait theory, personality can be broken down into a limited number of traits, which are present in each individual to a greater or lesser degree. This approach is highly compatible with the quantitative psychometric approach to personality testing.
Trait	An enduring personality characteristic that tends to lead to certain behaviors is called a trait. The term trait also means a genetically inherited feature of an organism.
Existentialism	The view that people are completely free and responsible for their own behavior is existentialism.
Humanistic	Humanistic refers to any system of thought focused on subjective experience and human problems and potentials.
Trial and error	Trial and error is an approach to problem solving in which one solution after another is tried in no particular order until an answer is found.
Determinism	Determinism is the philosophical proposition that every event, including human cognition and action, is causally determined by an unbroken chain of prior occurrences.
Vaihinger	Vaihinger argued that human beings can never really know the underlying reality of the world, and that as a result we construct systems of thought and then assume that these match reality.
Adler	Adler argued that human personality could be explained teleologically, separate strands dominated by the guiding purpose of the individual's unconscious self ideal to convert feelings of inferiority to superiority (or rather completeness). The desires of the self ideal were countered by social and ethical demands.
Introvert	Introvert refers to a person whose attention is focused inward; a shy, reserved, timid person.
Introversion	A personality trait characterized by intense imagination and a tendency to inhibit impulses is called introversion.
Superordinate	A hypernym is a word whose extension includes the extension of the word of which it is a hypernym. A word that is more generic or broad than another given word. Another term for a hypernym is a superordinate.
Modulation	Modulation is the process of varying a carrier signal, typically a sinusoidal signal, in order to use that signal to convey information.
Stimulus	A change in an environmental condition that elicits a response is a stimulus.
Metaphor	A metaphor is a rhetorical trope where a comparison is made between two seemingly unrelated subjects
Social cognitive theory	Social cognitive theory defines human behavior as a triadic, dynamic, and reciprocal interaction of personal factors, behavior, and the environment. Response consequences of a behavior are used to form expectations of behavioral outcomes. It is the ability to form these expectations that give humans the capability to predict the outcomes of their behavior, before the behavior is performed.

Chapter 13. George Kelly

Chapter 13. George Kelly

Anxiety	Anxiety is a complex combination of the feeling of fear, apprehension and worry often accompanied by physical sensations such as palpitations, chest pain and/or shortness of breath.
Elaboration	The extensiveness of processing at any given level of memory is called elaboration. The use of elaboration changes developmentally. Adolescents are more likely to use elaboration spontaneously than children.
Perception	Perception is the process of acquiring, interpreting, selecting, and organizing sensory information.
Repression	A defense mechanism, repression involves moving thoughts unacceptable to the ego into the unconscious, where they cannot be easily accessed.
Assimilation	According to Piaget, assimilation is the process of the organism interacting with the environment given the organism's cognitive structure. Assimilation is reuse of schemas to fit new information.
Learning	Learning is a relatively permanent change in behavior that results from experience. Thus, to attribute a behavioral change to learning, the change must be relatively permanent and must result from experience.
Classical conditioning	Classical conditioning is a simple form of learning in which an organism comes to associate or anticipate events. A neutral stimulus comes to evoke the response usually evoked by a natural or unconditioned stimulus by being paired repeatedly with the unconditioned stimulus.
Pavlov	Pavlov first described the phenomenon now known as classical conditioning in experiments with dogs.
Drive reduction	Drive reduction theories are based on the need-state. Drive activates behavior. Reinforcement occurs whenever drive is reduced, leading to learning of whatever response solves the need. Thus the reduction in need serves as reinforcement and produces reinforcement of the response that leads to it.
Punishment	Punishment is the addtion of a stimulus that reduces the frequency of a response, or the removal of a stimulus that results in a reduction of the response.
Attitude	An enduring mental representation of a person, place, or thing that evokes an emotional response and related behavior is called attitude.
Idiographic	An idiographic investigation studies the characteristics of an individual in depth.
Allport	Allport was a trait theorist. Those traits he believed to predominate a person's personality were called central traits. Traits such that one could be indentifed by the trait, were referred to as cardinal traits. Central traits and cardinal traits are influenced by environmental factors.
Clinician	A health professional authorized to provide services to people suffering from one or more pathologies is a clinician.
Paradigm	Paradigm refers to the set of practices that defines a scientific discipline during a particular period of time. It provides a framework from which to conduct research, it ensures that a certain range of phenomena, those on which the paradigm focuses, are explored thoroughly. Itmay also blind scientists to other, perhaps more fruitful, ways of dealing with their subject matter.
Kuhn	Kuhn is most famous for his book The Structure of Scientific Revolutions in which he presented the idea that science does not evolve gradually toward truth, but instead undergoes periodic revolutions which he calls "paradigm shifts."
Attention	Attention is the cognitive process of selectively concentrating on one thing while ignoring

Chapter 13. George Kelly

Chapter 13. George Kelly

other things. Psychologists have labeled three types of attention: sustained attention, selective attention, and divided attention.

Empirical	Empirical means the use of working hypotheses which are capable of being disproved using observation or experiment.
Fisher	Fisher was a eugenicist, evolutionary biologist, geneticist and statistician. He has been described as "The greatest of Darwin's successors", and a genius who almost single-handedly created the foundations for modern statistical science inventing the techniques of maximum likelihood and analysis of variance.
Psychoanalyst	A psychoanalyst is a specially trained therapist who attempts to treat the individual by uncovering and revealing to the individual otherwise subconscious factors that are contributing to some undesirable behavior.
Self-actualization	Self-actualization (a term originated by Kurt Goldstein) is the instinctual need of a human to make the most of their unique abilities. Maslow described it as follows: Self Actualization is the intrinsic growth of what is already in the organism, or more accurately, of what the organism is.
Habit	A habit is a response that has become completely separated from its eliciting stimulus. Early learning theorists used the term to describe S-R associations, however not all S-R associations become a habit, rather many are extinguished after reinforcement is withdrawn.
Variable	A variable refers to a measurable factor, characteristic, or attribute of an individual or a system.
Premise	A premise is a statement presumed true within the context of a discourse, especially of a logical argument.
Individuality	According to Cooper, individuality consists of two dimensions: self-assertion and separateness.
Dichotomy	A dichotomy is the division of a proposition into two parts which are both mutually exclusive – i.e. both cannot be simultaneously true – and jointly exhaustive – i.e. they cover the full range of possible outcomes. They are often contrasting and spoken of as "opposites".
Industrial-organizational psychology	Industrial-organizational psychology is the study of the behavior of people in the workplace. Industrial and organizational psychology attempts to apply psychological results and methods to aid workers and organizations.
Social psychology	Social psychology is the study of the nature and causes of human social behavior, with an emphasis on how people think towards each other and how they relate to each other.
Behavior therapy	Behavior therapy refers to the systematic application of the principles of learning to direct modification of a client's problem behaviors.
Schizophrenia	Schizophrenia is characterized by persistent defects in the perception or expression of reality. A person suffering from untreated schizophrenia typically demonstrates grossly disorganized thinking, and may also experience delusions or auditory hallucinations
George Kelly	George Kelly developed his major contribution to the psychology of personality, The Psychology of Personal Constructs in 1955 and achieved immediate international recognition. He worked in clinical school psychology, developing a program of traveling clinics which also served as a training ground for his students.
Anorexia	Anorexia nervosa is an eating disorder characterized by voluntary starvation and exercise stress.
Group therapy	Group therapy is a form of psychotherapy during which one or several therapists treat a small group of clients together as a group. This may be more cost effective than individual

Chapter 13. George Kelly

	therapy, and possibly even more effective.
Developmental psychology	The branch of psychology that studies the patterns of growth and change occurring throughout life is referred to as developmental psychology.
Human nature	Human nature is the fundamental nature and substance of humans, as well as the range of human behavior that is believed to be invariant over long periods of time and across very different cultural contexts.

Chapter 13. George Kelly

Chapter 14. Carl Rogers

Attitude	An enduring mental representation of a person, place, or thing that evokes an emotional response and related behavior is called attitude.
Carl Rogers	Carl Rogers was instrumental in the development of non-directive psychotherapy, also known as "client-centered" psychotherapy. Rogers' basic tenets were unconditional positive regard, genuineness, and empathic understanding, with each demonstrated by the counselor.
Species	Species refers to a reproductively isolated breeding population.
Behaviorism	The school of psychology that defines psychology as the study of observable behavior and studies relationships between stimuli and responses is called behaviorism. Behaviorism relied heavily on animal research and stated the same principles governed the behavior of both nonhumans and humans.
Educational psychology	Educational psychology is the study of how children and adults learn, the effectiveness of various educational strategies and tactics, and how schools function as organizations.
Psychotherapy	Psychotherapy is a set of techniques based on psychological principles intended to improve mental health, emotional or behavioral issues.
Personality	Personality refers to the pattern of enduring characteristics that differentiates a person, the patterns of behaviors that make each individual unique.
Society	The social sciences use the term society to mean a group of people that form a semi-closed (or semi-open) social system, in which most interactions are with other individuals belonging to the group.
Adler	Adler argued that human personality could be explained teleologically, separate strands dominated by the guiding purpose of the individual's unconscious self ideal to convert feelings of inferiority to superiority (or rather completeness). The desires of the self ideal were countered by social and ethical demands.
Clinical psychology	Clinical psychology is involved in the diagnosis, assessment, and treatment of patients with mental or behavioral disorders, and conducts research in these various areas.
Psychoanalysis	Psychoanalysis refers to the school of psychology that emphasizes the importance of unconscious motives and conflicts as determinants of human behavior. It was Freud's method of exploring human personality.
Encounter group	A type of group that fosters self-awareness by focusing on how group members relate to one another in a setting that encourages open expression of feelings is called an encounter group.
Self-actualization	Self-actualization (a term originated by Kurt Goldstein) is the instinctual need of a human to make the most of their unique abilities. Maslow described it as follows: Self Actualization is the intrinsic growth of what is already in the organism, or more accurately, of what the organism is.
Innate	Innate behavior is not learned or influenced by the environment, rather, it is present or predisposed at birth.
Human nature	Human nature is the fundamental nature and substance of humans, as well as the range of human behavior that is believed to be invariant over long periods of time and across very different cultural contexts.
Motives	Needs or desires that energize and direct behavior toward a goal are motives.
Humanistic	Humanistic refers to any system of thought focused on subjective experience and human problems and potentials.
Humanistic	Humanistic psychology refers to the school of psychology that focuses on the uniqueness of

Chapter 14. Carl Rogers

Chapter 14. Carl Rogers

psychology	human beings and their capacity for choice, growth, and psychological health.
George Kelly	George Kelly developed his major contribution to the psychology of personality, The Psychology of Personal Constructs in 1955 and achieved immediate international recognition. He worked in clinical school psychology, developing a program of traveling clinics which also served as a training ground for his students.
Rollo May	Rollo May was the best known American existential psychologist, authoring the influential book Love and Will in 1969. He differs from other humanistic psychologists in showing a sharper awareness of the tragic dimensions of human existence.
Allport	Allport was a trait theorist. Those traits he believed to predominate a person's personality were called central traits. Traits such that one could be indentifed by the trait, were referred to as cardinal traits. Central traits and cardinal traits are influenced by environmental factors.
Maslow	Maslow is mostly noted today for his proposal of a hierarchy of human needs which he often presented as a pyramid. Maslow was an instrumental player in the formation of the humanistic movement, also known as the third force in psychology.
Feedback	Feedback refers to information returned to a person about the effects a response has had.
Learning	Learning is a relatively permanent change in behavior that results from experience. Thus, to attribute a behavioral change to learning, the change must be relatively permanent and must result from experience.
Emotion	An emotion is a mental states that arise spontaneously, rather than through conscious effort. They are often accompanied by physiological changes.
Construct	A generalized concept, such as anxiety or gravity, is a construct.
Socialization	Social rules and social relations are created, communicated, and changed in verbal and nonverbal ways creating social complexity useful in identifying outsiders and intelligent breeding partners. The process of learning these skills is called socialization.
Superego	Frued's third psychic structure, which functions as a moral guardian and sets forth high standards for behavior is the superego.
Unconditional positive regard	Unqualified caring and nonjudgmental acceptance of another is called unconditional positive regard.
Variance	The degree to which scores differ among individuals in a distribution of scores is the variance.
Anxiety	Anxiety is a complex combination of the feeling of fear, apprehension and worry often accompanied by physical sensations such as palpitations, chest pain and/or shortness of breath.
Denial	Denial is a psychological defense mechanism in which a person faced with a fact that is uncomfortable or painful to accept rejects it instead, insisting that it is not true despite what may be overwhelming evidence.
Symbolization	In Bandura's social cognitive theory, the ability to think about one's social behavior in terms of words and images is referred to as symbolization. Symbolization allows us to translate a transient experience into a guide for future action.
Self-understanding	Self-understanding is a child's cognitive representation of the self, the substance and content of the child's self-conceptions.
Self-concept	Self-concept refers to domain-specific evaluations of the self where a domain may be academics, athletics, etc.

Chapter 14. Carl Rogers

Chapter 14. Carl Rogers

Hypothesis	A specific statement about behavior or mental processes that is testable through research is a hypothesis.
Nondirective therapy	Nondirective therapy is an approach in which the therapist acts to facilitate growth, giving understanding and support rather than proposing solutions, answering questions, or actively directing the course of therapy.
Evolution	Commonly used to refer to gradual change, evolution is the change in the frequency of alleles within a population from one generation to the next. This change may be caused by different mechanisms, including natural selection, genetic drift, or changes in population (gene flow).
Empathic understanding	Empathic understanding refers to ability to perceive a client's feelings from the client's frame of reference.
Biological needs	Beyond physiological needs for survival, the next level are motivations that have an obvious biological basis but are not required for the immediate survival of the organism. These biological needs include the powerful motivations for sex, parenting and aggression.
Empathy	Empathy is the recognition and understanding of the states of mind, including beliefs, desires and particularly emotions of others without injecting your own.
Adaptation	Adaptation is a lowering of sensitivity to a stimulus following prolonged exposure to that stimulus. Behavioral adaptations are special ways a particular organism behaves to survive in its natural habitat.
Creativity	Creativity is the ability to think about something in novel and unusual ways and come up with unique solutions to problems. It involves divergent thinking, having many solutions or views to a problem.
Subjective experience	Subjective experience refers to reality as it is perceived and interpreted, not as it exists objectively.
Q-sort technique	The Q-sort technique is a standardized procedure for assessing the self-concept. It entails making ranked comparative judgments of statements about one's self.
Normal distribution	A normal distribution is a symmetrical distribution of scores that is assumed to reflect chance fluctuations; approximately 68% of cases lie within a single standard deviation of the mean.
Trait	An enduring personality characteristic that tends to lead to certain behaviors is called a trait. The term trait also means a genetically inherited feature of an organism.
Correlation coefficient	Correlation coefficient refers to a number from +1.00 to -1.00 that expresses the direction and extent of the relationship between two variables. The closer to 1, the stronger the relationship. The sign, + or -, indicates the direction.
American Psychological Association	The American Psychological Association is a professional organization representing psychology in the US. The mission statement is to "advance psychology as a science and profession and as a means of promoting health, education , and human welfare".
Skinner	Skinner conducted research on shaping behavior through positive and negative reinforcement, and demonstrated operant conditioning, a technique which he developed in contrast with classical conditioning.
Reinforcement contingencies	The circumstances or rules that determine whether responses lead to the presentation of reinforcers are referred to as reinforcement contingencies. Skinner defined culture as a set of reinforcement contingencies.
Openness to Experience	Openness to Experience, one of the big-five traits, describes a dimension of cognitive style that distinguishes imaginative, creative people from down-to-earth, conventional people.

Go to Cram101.com for the Practice Tests for this Chapter.

Chapter 14. Carl Rogers

Chapter 14. Carl Rogers

Learning to learn	Learning to learn is a phenomenon where performance on later tasks is enhanced as a result of performance on earlier tasks, in which a general set of rules or approaches to a problem is acquired.
Statistics	Statistics is a type of data analysis which practice includes the planning, summarizing, and interpreting of observations of a system possibly followed by predicting or forecasting of future events based on a mathematical model of the system being observed.
Conformity	Conformity is the degree to which members of a group will change their behavior, views and attitudes to fit the views of the group. The group can influence members via unconscious processes or via overt social pressure on individuals.
Hypocrisy	Publicly advocating some attitude or behavior and then acting in a way that is inconsistent with this espoused attitude or behavior is called hypocrisy.
Empirical	Empirical means the use of working hypotheses which are capable of being disproved using observation or experiment.
Correlation	A statistical technique for determining the degree of association between two or more variables is referred to as correlation.
Control group	A group that does not receive the treatment effect in an experiment is referred to as the control group or sometimes as the comparison group.
Penis	The penis is the external male copulatory organ and the external male organ of urination. In humans, the penis is homologous to the female clitoris, as it develops from the same embryonic structure. It is capable of erection for use in copulation.
Theories	Theories are logically self-consistent models or frameworks describing the behavior of a certain natural or social phenomenon. They are broad explanations and predictions concerning phenomena of interest.
Clinical psychologist	A psychologist, usually with a Ph.D, whose training is in the diagnosis, treatment, or research of psychological and behavioral disorders is a clinical psychologist.
Role model	A person who serves as a positive example of desirable behavior is referred to as a role model.
Premise	A premise is a statement presumed true within the context of a discourse, especially of a logical argument.
Heuristic	A heuristic is a simple, efficient rule of thumb proposed to explain how people make decisions, come to judgments and solve problems, typically when facing complex problems or incomplete information. These rules work well under most circumstances, but in certain cases lead to systematic cognitive biases.
Sympathetic	The sympathetic nervous system activates what is often termed the "fight or flight response". It is an automatic regulation system, that is, one that operates without the intervention of conscious thought.
Client-Centered Therapy	Client-Centered Therapy was developed by Carl Rogers. It is based on the principal of talking therapy and is a non-directive approach. The therapist encourages the patient to express their feelings and does not suggest how the person might wish to change, but by listening and then mirroring back what the patient reveals to them, helps them to explore and understand their feelings for themselves.
Authoritarian	The term authoritarian is used to describe a style that enforces strong and sometimes oppressive measures against those in its sphere of influence, generally without attempts at gaining their consent.
Consciousness	The awareness of the sensations, thoughts, and feelings being experienced at a given moment

Chapter 14. Carl Rogers

	is called consciousness.
Perception	Perception is the process of acquiring, interpreting, selecting, and organizing sensory information.
Self-image	A person's self-image is the mental picture, generally of a kind that is quite resistant to change, that depicts not only details that are potentially available to objective investigation by others, but also items that have been learned by that person about himself or herself.

Chapter 14. Carl Rogers

Chapter 15. Abraham Maslow

Maslow	Maslow is mostly noted today for his proposal of a hierarchy of human needs which he often presented as a pyramid. Maslow was an instrumental player in the formation of the humanistic movement, also known as the third force in psychology.
Humanistic psychology	Humanistic psychology refers to the school of psychology that focuses on the uniqueness of human beings and their capacity for choice, growth, and psychological health.
Motivation	In psychology, motivation is the driving force (desire) behind all actions of an organism.
Titchener	Titchener attempted to classify the structures of the mind, not unlike the way a chemist breaks down chemicals into their component parts-water into hydrogen and oxygen for example. He conceived of hydrogen and oxygen as structures of a chemical compound, and sensations and thoughts as structures of the mind. This approach became known as structuralism.
Introspection	Introspection is the self report or consideration of one's own thoughts, perceptions and mental processes. Classic introspection was done through trained observers.
Behaviorism	The school of psychology that defines psychology as the study of observable behavior and studies relationships between stimuli and responses is called behaviorism. Behaviorism relied heavily on animal research and stated the same principles governed the behavior of both nonhumans and humans.
Harlow	Harlow and his famous wire and cloth surrogate mother monkey studies demonstrated that the need for affection created a stronger bond between mother and infant than did physical needs. He also found that the more discrimination problems the monkeys solved, the better they became at solving them.
Thorndike	Thorndike worked in animal behavior and the learning process leading to the theory of connectionism. Among his most famous contributions were his research on cats escaping from puzzle boxes, and his formulation of the Law of Effect.
Learning	Learning is a relatively permanent change in behavior that results from experience. Thus, to attribute a behavioral change to learning, the change must be relatively permanent and must result from experience.
Intelligence test	An intelligence test is a standardized means of assessing a person's current mental ability, for example, the Stanford-Binet test and the Wechsler Adult Intelligence Scale.
Stereotype	A stereotype is considered to be a group concept, held by one social group about another. They are often used in a negative or prejudicial sense and are frequently used to justify certain discriminatory behaviors. This allows powerful social groups to legitimize and protect their dominant position
Karen Horney	Karen Horney, a neo-Freudian, deviated from orthodox Freudian analysis by emphasizing environmental and cultural, rather than biological, factors in neurosis.
Wertheimer	His discovery of the phi phenomenon concerning the illusion of motion gave rise to the influential school of Gestalt psychology. In the latter part of his life, Wertheimer directed much of his attention to the problem of learning.
Adler	Adler argued that human personality could be explained teleologically, separate strands dominated by the guiding purpose of the individual's unconscious self ideal to convert feelings of inferiority to superiority (or rather completeness). The desires of the self ideal were countered by social and ethical demands.
Aristotle	Aristotle can be credited with the development of the first theory of learning. He concluded that ideas were generated in consciousness based on four principles of association: contiguity, similarity, contrast, and succession. In contrast to Plato, he believed that knowledge derived from sensory experience and was not inherited.

Chapter 15. Abraham Maslow

Chapter 15. Abraham Maslow

Spinoza	Spinoza was a determinist who held that absolutely everything that happens occurs through the operation of necessity. All behavior is fully determined, freedom being our capacity to know we are determined and to understand why we act as we do.
Psychoanalysis	Psychoanalysis refers to the school of psychology that emphasizes the importance of unconscious motives and conflicts as determinants of human behavior. It was Freud's method of exploring human personality.
Personality	Personality refers to the pattern of enduring characteristics that differentiates a person, the patterns of behaviors that make each individual unique.
Human nature	Human nature is the fundamental nature and substance of humans, as well as the range of human behavior that is believed to be invariant over long periods of time and across very different cultural contexts.
Intuition	Quick, impulsive thought that does not make use of formal logic or clear reasoning is referred to as intuition.
American Psychological Association	The American Psychological Association is a professional organization representing psychology in the US. The mission statement is to "advance psychology as a science and profession and as a means of promoting health, education, and human welfare".
Social psychology	Social psychology is the study of the nature and causes of human social behavior, with an emphasis on how people think towards each other and how they relate to each other.
Humanistic	Humanistic refers to any system of thought focused on subjective experience and human problems and potentials.
Allport	Allport was a trait theorist. Those traits he believed to predominate a person's personality were called central traits. Traits such that one could be indentifed by the trait, were referred to as cardinal traits. Central traits and cardinal traits are influenced by environmental factors.
Psychoanalytic	Freud's theory that unconscious forces act as determinants of personality is called psychoanalytic theory. The theory is a developmental theory characterized by critical stages of development.
Instinct	Instinct is the word used to describe inherent dispositions towards particular actions. They are generally an inherited pattern of responses or reactions to certain kinds of situations.
Habit	A habit is a response that has become completely separated from its eliciting stimulus. Early learning theorists used the term to describe S-R associations, however not all S-R associations become a habit, rather many are extinguished after reinforcement is withdrawn.
Reductionism	Reductionism holds that the nature of complex things can always be reduced to (be explained by) simpler or more fundamental things.
Creativity	Creativity is the ability to think about something in novel and unusual ways and come up with unique solutions to problems. It involves divergent thinking, having many solutions or views to a problem.
Hierarchy of needs	Maslow's hierarchy of needs is often depicted as a pyramid consisting of five levels: the four lower levels are grouped together as deficiency needs, while the top level is termed being needs. While our deficiency needs must be met, our being needs are continually shaping our behavior.
Senses	The senses are systems that consist of a sensory cell type that respond to a specific kind of physical energy, and that correspond to a defined region within the brain where the signals are received and interpreted.
Physiological	The easiest kinds of motivation to analyse, at least superficially, are those based upon

Chapter 15. Abraham Maslow

Chapter 15. Abraham Maslow

needs	obvious physiological needs. These include hunger, thirst, and escape from pain.
Motives	Needs or desires that energize and direct behavior toward a goal are motives.
Need for Affiliation	Need for Affiliation is a term introduced by David McClelland to describe a person's need to feel like he needs to belong to a group. These individuals require warm interpersonal relationships and approval from those in these relationships is very satisfying. People who value affiliation a lot tend to be good team members, but poor leaders.
Psychotherapy	Psychotherapy is a set of techniques based on psychological principles intended to improve mental health, emotional or behavioral issues.
Self-actualization	Self-actualization (a term originated by Kurt Goldstein) is the instinctual need of a human to make the most of their unique abilities. Maslow described it as follows: Self Actualization is the intrinsic growth of what is already in the organism, or more accurately, of what the organism is.
Self-esteem	Self-esteem refers to a person's subjective appraisal of himself or herself as intrinsically positive or negative to some degree.
Early childhood	Early childhood refers to the developmental period extending from the end of infancy to about 5 or 6 years of age; sometimes called the preschool years.
Fixation	Fixation in abnormal psychology is the state where an individual becomes obsessed with an attachment to another human, animal or inanimate object. Fixation in vision refers to maintaining the gaze in a constant direction. .
Society	The social sciences use the term society to mean a group of people that form a semi-closed (or semi-open) social system, in which most interactions are with other individuals belonging to the group.
Blocking	If the one of the two members of a compound stimulus fails to produce the CR due to an earlier conditioning of the other member of the compound stimulus, blocking has occurred.
Self-actualizing	Self-actualizing is the need of a human to make the most of their unique abilities.
Affect	A subjective feeling or emotional tone often accompanied by bodily expressions noticeable to others is called affect.
Perception	Perception is the process of acquiring, interpreting, selecting, and organizing sensory information.
Cognition	The intellectual processes through which information is obtained, transformed, stored, retrieved, and otherwise used is cognition.
Anxiety	Anxiety is a complex combination of the feeling of fear, apprehension and worry often accompanied by physical sensations such as palpitations, chest pain and/or shortness of breath.
Population	Population refers to all members of a well-defined group of organisms, events, or things.
Self-actualizer	One who is living creatively and making full use of his or her potentials is referred to as a self-actualizer.
William James	Functionalism as a psychology developed out of Pragmatism as a philosophy: To find the meaning of an idea, you have to look at its consequences. This led William James and his students towards an emphasis on cause and effect, prediction and control, and observation of environment and behavior, over the careful introspection of the Structuralists.
Peak experiences	Temporary moments of self-actualization are peak experiences.
Ecstasy	Ecstasy as an emotion is to be outside oneself, in a trancelike state in which an individual

Chapter 15. Abraham Maslow

Chapter 15. Abraham Maslow

	transcends ordinary consciousness and as a result has a heightened capacity for exceptional thought or experience. Ecstasy also refers to a relatively new hallucinogen that is chemically similar to mescaline and the amphetamines.
Friendship	The essentials of friendship are reciprocity and commitment between individuals who see themselves more or less as equals. Interaction between friends rests on a more equal power base than the interaction between children and adults.
Trait	An enduring personality characteristic that tends to lead to certain behaviors is called a trait. The term trait also means a genetically inherited feature of an organism.
Attitude	An enduring mental representation of a person, place, or thing that evokes an emotional response and related behavior is called attitude.
Ambivalence	The simultaneous holding of strong positive and negative emotional attitudes toward the same situation or person is called ambivalence.
Norms	In testing, standards of test performance that permit the comparison of one person's score on the test to the scores of others who have taken the same test are referred to as norms.
Dichotomy	A dichotomy is the division of a proposition into two parts which are both mutually exclusive – i.e. both cannot be simultaneously true – and jointly exhaustive – i.e. they cover the full range of possible outcomes. They are often contrasting and spoken of as "opposites".
Anatomy	Anatomy is the branch of biology that deals with the structure and organization of living things. It can be divided into animal anatomy (zootomy) and plant anatomy (phytonomy). Major branches of anatomy include comparative anatomy, histology, and human anatomy.
Free choice	Free choice refers to the ability to freely make choices that are not controlled by genetics, learning, or unconscious forces.
Brain	The brain controls and coordinates most movement, behavior and homeostatic body functions such as heartbeat, blood pressure, fluid balance and body temperature. Functions of the brain are responsible for cognition, emotion, memory, motor learning and other sorts of learning. The brain is primarily made up of two types of cells: glia and neurons.
Transpersonal psychology	Transpersonal psychology is a school of psychology that studies the transcendent, or spiritual dimensions of humanity. Among these factors we find such issues as self-development, peak experiences, mystical experiences and the possibility of development beyond traditional ego-boundaries.
Consciousness	The awareness of the sensations, thoughts, and feelings being experienced at a given moment is called consciousness.
Meditation	Meditation usually refers to a state in which the body is consciously relaxed and the mind is allowed to become calm and focused.
Empirical	Empirical means the use of working hypotheses which are capable of being disproved using observation or experiment.
Control group	A group that does not receive the treatment effect in an experiment is referred to as the control group or sometimes as the comparison group.
Group therapy	Group therapy is a form of psychotherapy during which one or several therapists treat a small group of clients together as a group. This may be more cost effective than individual therapy, and possibly even more effective.
Graham	Graham has conducted a number of studies that reveal stronger socioeconomic-status influences rather than ethnic influences in achievement.
Hypothesis	A specific statement about behavior or mental processes that is testable through research is

Chapter 15. Abraham Maslow

Chapter 15. Abraham Maslow

	a hypothesis.
Positive relationship	Statistically, a positive relationship refers to a mathematical relationship in which increases in one measure are matched by increases in the other.
Sullivan	Sullivan developed the Self System, a configuration of the personality traits developed in childhood and reinforced by positive affirmation and the security operations developed in childhood to avoid anxiety and threats to self-esteem.
Industrial-organizational psychology	Industrial-organizational psychology is the study of the behavior of people in the workplace. Industrial and organizational psychology attempts to apply psychological results and methods to aid workers and organizations.
Attention	Attention is the cognitive process of selectively concentrating on one thing while ignoring other things. Psychologists have labeled three types of attention: sustained attention, selective attention, and divided attention.
Reflection	Reflection is the process of rephrasing or repeating thoughts and feelings expressed, making the person more aware of what they are saying or thinking.
Insight	Insight refers to a sudden awareness of the relationships among various elements that had previously appeared to be independent of one another.
Csikszentmihalyi	Csikszentmihalyi is noted for his work in the study of happiness, creativity, subjective well-being, and fun, but is best known for his having been the architect of the notion of flow: "... people are most happy when they are in a state of flow--a Zen-like state of total oneness...".
Pathology	Pathology is the study of the processes underlying disease and other forms of illness, harmful abnormality, or dysfunction.
Innate	Innate behavior is not learned or influenced by the environment, rather, it is present or predisposed at birth.
Theories	Theories are logically self-consistent models or frameworks describing the behavior of a certain natural or social phenomenon. They are broad explanations and predictions concerning phenomena of interest.
Jung	Jung was in some aspects a response to Sigmund Freud's psychoanalysis. He proposed and developed the concepts of the extroverted and introverted personality, archetypes, and the collective unconscious. His work has been influential in psychiatry and in the study of religion, literature, and related fields.
Autonomy	Autonomy is the condition of something that does not depend on anything else.
Physiological drives	Unlearned drives with a biological basis, such as hunger, thirst, and avoidance of pain are called physiological drives. Physiological drives are homeostatic where action is directed to return the organsim to a state of equlibrium.
Psychoanalyst	A psychoanalyst is a specially trained therapist who attempts to treat the individual by uncovering and revealing to the individual otherwise subconscious factors that are contributing to some undesirable behavior.
Utopian	An ideal vision of society is a utopian society.
Evolution	Commonly used to refer to gradual change, evolution is the change in the frequency of alleles within a population from one generation to the next. This change may be caused by different mechanisms, including natural selection, genetic drift, or changes in population (gene flow).
Scientific method	Psychologists gather data in order to describe, understand, predict, and control behavior. Scientific method refers to an approach that can be used to discover accurate information. It

Chapter 15. Abraham Maslow

	includes these steps: understand the problem, collect data, draw conclusions, and revise research conclusions.
Psychological disorder	Mental processes and/or behavior patterns that cause emotional distress and/or substantial impairment in functioning is a psychological disorder.

Chapter 15. Abraham Maslow

Chapter 16. Rollo Reese May

Existential psychology	Existential psychology is partly based on the belief that human beings are alone in the world. This aloneness leads to feelings of meaninglessness which can be overcome only by creating one's own values and meanings
Humanistic	Humanistic refers to any system of thought focused on subjective experience and human problems and potentials.
Schizophrenia	Schizophrenia is characterized by persistent defects in the perception or expression of reality. A person suffering from untreated schizophrenia typically demonstrates grossly disorganized thinking, and may also experience delusions or auditory hallucinations
Nervous breakdown	Nervous breakdown is often used by laymen to describe a sudden and acute attack of mental illness—for instance, clinical depression or anxiety disorder—in a previously outwardly healthy person. Breakdowns are the result of chronic and unrelenting nervous strain, and not a sign of weakness.
Insight	Insight refers to a sudden awareness of the relationships among various elements that had previously appeared to be independent of one another.
Learning	Learning is a relatively permanent change in behavior that results from experience. Thus, to attribute a behavioral change to learning, the change must be relatively permanent and must result from experience.
Adler	Adler argued that human personality could be explained teleologically, separate strands dominated by the guiding purpose of the individual's unconscious self ideal to convert feelings of inferiority to superiority (or rather completeness). The desires of the self ideal were countered by social and ethical demands.
Counselor	A counselor is a mental health professional who specializes in helping people with problems not involving serious mental disorders.
Human nature	Human nature is the fundamental nature and substance of humans, as well as the range of human behavior that is believed to be invariant over long periods of time and across very different cultural contexts.
Obedience	Obedience is the willingness to follow the will of others. Humans have been shown to be surprisingly obedient in the presence of perceived legitimate authority figures, as demonstrated by the Milgram experiment in the 1960s.
Psychoanalysis	Psychoanalysis refers to the school of psychology that emphasizes the importance of unconscious motives and conflicts as determinants of human behavior. It was Freud's method of exploring human personality.
Sullivan	Sullivan developed the Self System, a configuration of the personality traits developed in childhood and reinforced by positive affirmation and the security operations developed in childhood to avoid anxiety and threats to self-esteem.
Clinical psychology	Clinical psychology is involved in the diagnosis, assessment, and treatment of patients with mental or behavioral disorders, and conducts research in these various areas.
Psychoanalyst	A psychoanalyst is a specially trained therapist who attempts to treat the individual by uncovering and revealing to the individual otherwise subconscious factors that are contributing to some undesirable behavior.
Kierkegaard	Kierkegaard has achieved general recognition as the first existentialist philosopher, though some new research shows this may be a more difficult connection than previously thought.
Anxiety	Anxiety is a complex combination of the feeling of fear, apprehension and worry often accompanied by physical sensations such as palpitations, chest pain and/or shortness of breath.

Go to Cram101.com for the Practice Tests for this Chapter.

Chapter 16. Rollo Reese May

Chapter 16. Rollo Reese May

American Psychological Association	The American Psychological Association is a professional organization representing psychology in the US. The mission statement is to "advance psychology as a science and profession and as a means of promoting health, education , and human welfare".
Clinical psychologist	A psychologist, usually with a Ph.D, whose training is in the diagnosis, treatment, or research of psychological and behavioral disorders is a clinical psychologist.
Society	The social sciences use the term society to mean a group of people that form a semi-closed (or semi-open) social system, in which most interactions are with other individuals belonging to the group.
Rollo May	Rollo May was the best known American existential psychologist, authoring the influential book Love and Will in 1969. He differs from other humanistic psychologists in showing a sharper awareness of the tragic dimensions of human existence.
Existentialism	The view that people are completely free and responsible for their own behavior is existentialism.
Personality	Personality refers to the pattern of enduring characteristics that differentiates a person, the patterns of behaviors that make each individual unique.
Binswanger	Binswanger is considered the founder of existential psychology. In the early 1920s he turned increasingly towards an existential rather than Freudian perspective, so that by the early 1930s he had become the first existential therapist.
Heidegger	Heidegger is regarded as a major influence on existentialism. He focused on the phenomenon of intentionality. Human behavior is intentional insofar as it is directed at some object or end (all building is building of something, all talking is talking about something, etc).
Nietzsche	Nietzsche in his own estimation was a psychologist. His works helped to reinforce not only agnostic trends that followed Enlightenment thinkers, and the evolutionary theory of Charles Darwin, but also the interpretations of human behavior by Sigmund Freud.
Consciousness	The awareness of the sensations, thoughts, and feelings being experienced at a given moment is called consciousness.
Genetics	Genetics is the science of genes, heredity, and the variation of organisms.
Phenomenology	Phenomenology is the study of subjective mental experiences; a theme of humanistic theories of personality. It studies meaningful, intact mental events without dividing them for further analysis.
Free will	The idea that human beings are capable of freely making choices or decisions is free will.
Dichotomy	A dichotomy is the division of a proposition into two parts which are both mutually exclusive – i.e. both cannot be simultaneously true – and jointly exhaustive – i.e. they cover the full range of possible outcomes. They are often contrasting and spoken of as "opposites".
Determinism	Determinism is the philosophical proposition that every event, including human cognition and action, is causally determined by an unbroken chain of prior occurrences.
Stimulus	A change in an environmental condition that elicits a response is a stimulus.
Skinner	Skinner conducted research on shaping behavior through positive and negative reinforcement, and demonstrated operant conditioning, a technique which he developed in contrast with classical conditioning.
Emotion	An emotion is a mental states that arise spontaneously, rather than through conscious effort. They are often accompanied by physiological changes.
Intentionality	Brentano defined intentionality as the main characteristic of "psychical phenomena," by which they could be distinguished from "physical phenomena.". Every mental phenomenon, every

Go to Cram101.com for the Practice Tests for this Chapter.

Chapter 16. Rollo Reese May

	psychological act has a content, is directed at an object (the intentional object).
Subjective experience	Subjective experience refers to reality as it is perceived and interpreted, not as it exists objectively.
Senses	The senses are systems that consist of a sensory cell type that respond to a specific kind of physical energy, and that correspond to a defined region within the brain where the signals are received and interpreted.
Guilt	Guilt describes many concepts related to a negative emotion or condition caused by actions which are believed to be, morally wrong. According to Freud, the avoidance of guilt is the basis for moral behavior.
Neurotic anxiety	Neurotic anxiety refers to, in psychoanalytic theory, a fear of the consequences of expressing previously punished and repressed id impulses; more generally, unrealistic fear.
Conformity	Conformity is the degree to which members of a group will change their behavior, views and attitudes to fit the views of the group. The group can influence members via unconscious processes or via overt social pressure on individuals.
Repression	A defense mechanism, repression involves moving thoughts unacceptable to the ego into the unconscious, where they cannot be easily accessed.
Intrapsychic conflict	In psychoanalysis, the struggles among the id, ego, and superego are an intrapsychic conflict.
Oedipus conflict	For Freud, a child's sexual interest in his or her opposite-sex parent, typically resolved through identification with the same-sex parent, is an Oedipus conflict.
Identity crisis	Erikson coinded the term identity crisis: "...a psychosocial state or condition of disorientation and role confusion occurring especially in adolescents as a result of conflicting internal and external experiences, pressures, and expectations and often producing acute anxiety."
Rote	Rote learning, is a learning technique which avoids grasping the inner complexities and inferences of the subject that is being learned and instead focuses on memorizing the material so that it can be recalled by the learner exactly the way it was read or heard.
Eros	In Freudian psychology, Eros is the life instinct innate in all humans. It is the desire to create life and favours productivity and construction. Eros battles against the destructive death instinct of Thanatos.
Construct	A generalized concept, such as anxiety or gravity, is a construct.
Psychotherapy	Psychotherapy is a set of techniques based on psychological principles intended to improve mental health, emotional or behavioral issues.
Self-actualization	Self-actualization (a term originated by Kurt Goldstein) is the instinctual need of a human to make the most of their unique abilities. Maslow described it as follows: Self Actualization is the intrinsic growth of what is already in the organism, or more accurately, of what the organism is.
Maslow	Maslow is mostly noted today for his proposal of a hierarchy of human needs which he often presented as a pyramid. Maslow was an instrumental player in the formation of the humanistic movement, also known as the third force in psychology.
Symbolization	In Bandura's social cognitive theory, the ability to think about one's social behavior in terms of words and images is referred to as symbolization. Symbolization allows us to translate a transient experience into a guide for future action.
Sociobiology	Sociobiology is a synthesis of scientific disciplines that attempts to explain behavior in

Chapter 16. Rollo Reese May

Chapter 16. Rollo Reese May

	all species by considering the evolutionary advantages of social behaviors.
Vaihinger	Vaihinger argued that human beings can never really know the underlying reality of the world, and that as a result we construct systems of thought and then assume that these match reality.
Archetype	The archetype is a concept of psychologist Carl Jung. They are innate prototypes for ideas, which may subsequently become involved in the interpretation of observed phenomena. A group of memories and interpretations closely associated with an archetype is called a complex.
Jung	Jung was in some aspects a response to Sigmund Freud's psychoanalysis. He proposed and developed the concepts of the extroverted and introverted personality, archetypes, and the collective unconscious. His work has been influential in psychiatry and in the study of religion, literature, and related fields.
Drug addiction	Drug addiction, or substance dependence is the compulsive use of drugs, to the point where the user has no effective choice but to continue use.
Depression	In everyday language depression refers to any downturn in mood, which may be relatively transitory and perhaps due to something trivial. This is differentiated from Clinical depression which is marked by symptoms that last two weeks or more and are so severe that they interfere with daily living.
Suicide	Suicide behavior is rare in childhood but escalates in adolescence. The suicide rate increases in a linear fashion from adolescence through late adulthood.
Personal identity	The portion of the self-concept that pertains to the self as a distinct, separate individual is called personal identity.
Individualist	A person who defines the self in terms of personal traits and gives priority to personal goals is an individualist.
Trait	An enduring personality characteristic that tends to lead to certain behaviors is called a trait. The term trait also means a genetically inherited feature of an organism.
Brain	The brain controls and coordinates most movement, behavior and homeostatic body functions such as heartbeat, blood pressure, fluid balance and body temperature. Functions of the brain are responsible for cognition, emotion, memory, motor learning and other sorts of learning. The brain is primarily made up of two types of cells: glia and neurons.
Habit	A habit is a response that has become completely separated from its eliciting stimulus. Early learning theorists used the term to describe S-R associations, however not all S-R associations become a habit, rather many are extinguished after reinforcement is withdrawn.
Elementism	Elementism is study of complex phenomena in terms of their basic parts or elements and the laws that describe them.
Empirical	Empirical means the use of working hypotheses which are capable of being disproved using observation or experiment.
Physiology	The study of the functions and activities of living cells, tissues, and organs and of the physical and chemical phenomena involved is referred to as physiology.
Friendship	The essentials of friendship are reciprocity and commitment between individuals who see themselves more or less as equals. Interaction between friends rests on a more equal power base than the interaction between children and adults.
Existential therapy	Existential therapy is partly based on the belief that human beings are alone in the world. This aloneness leads to feelings of meaninglessness which can be overcome only by creating one's own values and meanings. We have the power to create because we have the freedom to choose.

Chapter 16. Rollo Reese May

Chapter 16. Rollo Reese May

Individualism	Individualism refers to putting personal goals ahead of group goals and defining one's identity in terms of personal attributes rather than group memberships.
Self-worth	In psychology, self-esteem or self-worth refers to a person's subjective appraisal of himself or herself as intrinsically positive or negative to some degree.
Self-alienation	Self-alienation is an anti-evolutionary trend in which a personality withdraws from a wider boundary of relationships to a smaller one. In the extreme, the person retracts his boundaries to within himself.
Assertiveness	Assertiveness basically means the ability to express your thoughts and feelings in a way that clearly states your needs and keeps the lines of communication open with the other.
Individuality	According to Cooper, individuality consists of two dimensions: self-assertion and separateness.
Self-awareness	Realization that one's existence and functioning are separate from those of other people and things is called self-awareness.

Chapter 16. Rollo Reese May

Chapter 17. A Final Word

Personality	Personality refers to the pattern of enduring characteristics that differentiates a person, the patterns of behaviors that make each individual unique.
Paradigm	Paradigm refers to the set of practices that defines a scientific discipline during a particular period of time. It provides a framework from which to conduct research, it ensures that a certain range of phenomena, those on which the paradigm focuses, are explored thoroughly. It may also blind scientists to other, perhaps more fruitful, ways of dealing with their subject matter.
Theories	Theories are logically self-consistent models or frameworks describing the behavior of a certain natural or social phenomenon. They are broad explanations and predictions concerning phenomena of interest.
Individuality	According to Cooper, individuality consists of two dimensions: self-assertion and separateness.
Intuition	Quick, impulsive thought that does not make use of formal logic or clear reasoning is referred to as intuition.
Empirical	Empirical means the use of working hypotheses which are capable of being disproved using observation or experiment.

Go to **Cram101.com** for the Practice Tests for this Chapter.

Chapter 17. A Final Word